TRANSATLANTIC CRISIS

Europe & America in the '70s

TRANSATLANTIC CRISIS

Europe & America in the '70s

edited by
Joseph Godson

First published in Great Britain
in 1974 by Alcove Press Limited,
59 St. Martin's Lane, London WC2N 4JS

Printed in Great Britain
by Watmoughs Limited,
Bradford and London

ISBN: 0 85657 030 3

Foreword

This book reproduces, with later additions and expansions, the texts of a series of articles published between April and June 1974, in the *International Herald Tribune*. The series was conceived in connection with the twenty-fifth anniversary of the Atlantic Alliance and the political, economic and security problems and differences which have arisen of late between the United States and Europe.

While the Ottawa declaration signed in Brussels by members of the Alliance in early summer may have brought to an end certain aspects of the quarrel between them, it would be quite unrealistic to imagine that any of the underlying problems, notably those of European-American relations, have been resolved.

I am naturally most grateful to the authors on both sides of the ocean for their thoughtful contributions which, it is hoped, will stimulate further discussion of some of the issues that are likely to plague the West in the months and years ahead.

I am especially grateful to Dr Joseph Luns for taking time out to launch this book by writing the introduction.

J.G.

Contents

Introduction

by Joseph Luns

It is sometimes said that the North Atlantic Alliance is the victim of its own success, that, having preserved peace in its area since its inception twenty-five years ago, it has increasingly come to be taken for granted or even thought of as superfluous. There certainly seems to be a temptation to conclude that, as world peace finally rests on the balance of the two super powers' strategic nuclear deterrent, there is only a limited role for Europe to play.

These views are, however, totally and dangerously wrong. From its earliest days, it has been a task of the Alliance, which it has manifestly succeeded in carrying out, not only to shield its members from overt aggression but also from politico-military pressures designed to limit their freedom of action or even bring about a basic change to the nature of their societies.

Under the protection of the Alliance, Western Europe has recovered from the devastation of war and gone on to prosper and develop in its own chosen way. Thus, for example, we have seen the creation and expansion of the European Community made possible by the security provided by the Alliance for

Western Europe. Then again, a strong alliance linking Western Europe and North America has led to an increasing willingness on the part of the Soviet Union to relax confrontation in favour of negotiation. There has been a first SALT agreement, though its lasting significance will depend on the outcome of SALT II. An important improvement in relations between the Federal Republic of Germany and the Soviet Union and other Eastern countries has been achieved as a result of the German Government's *Ostpolitik*, based, as the Federal Government has always stressed, on their *Westpolitik* which in essence means on the policy of the Atlantic partnership. The Soviet Union has finally been persuaded, after the West had long pressed for such talks, to begin negotiations on mutual and balanced force reductions in Central Europe. A European security conference has been meeting for about a year without significant results yet. We still hope that the Conference will yield more than empty slogans.

At the time of writing (June 1974) these negotiations are either still incomplete or have yet to lead to concrete results. Their value in increasing contact and rebuilding confidence between the two sides should not be underestimated, nor should we make the mistake of concluding that a new era of East-West relations has already arrived. It is impossible to overlook the fact that while participating in these negotiations, the Soviet Union has gone on increasing its forces. As Mr Roy Mason points out in his contribution to this collection, they have built up a strategic nuclear force to the point where they have parity with the United States. And despite the fact that, unlike Europe, they do not depend on the world's sea lanes for vital supplies, they have built the second largest battle fleet in the world. They do not seriously seek to disguise that the main purpose of this fleet is to give them the capacity to exercise political influence through the world-wide use of naval power.

I may also refer to the article by Mr Schlesinger, in which he writes that Soviet defense spending since 1960 has risen an average of three per cent per year in real terms. Soviet armed forces have increased, he adds, by more than one million—1·5 million in his estimate—during those years.

We are therefore not faced with any very compelling evidence that the Soviet Union has abandoned the concept of the threat or even the use of force as an instrument of policy should a suitable opportunity occur. And how easily and quickly such occasions can arise was illustrated only recently by the Middle East war. This therefore is clearly not the moment to reduce our defense effort nor to undermine the deterrent. During a period of strategic nuclear parity, it has become more essential than ever to have adequate conventional forces to match those of the other side. For politico-military power cannot easily or safely be countered by a nuclear deterrent alone. There must be the possibility of responding flexibly, which means essentially at an appropriate military level, to a whole range of possible threats to the political independence, territorial integrity and sovereignty of the countries of the Alliance.

It is for this reason that I am greatly disturbed by increasing evidence of a reluctance among some sectors of public opinion to see sufficient resources allocated to the Alliance's conventional defense effort. It should most especially be borne in mind that in a period of inflation, greatly exacerbated by the oil crisis, considerable pressures will be placed on defense budgets. Any member country that succumbs and cuts its conventional forces is most unlikely to see another nation move in to fill the gap, but, on the contrary, will more likely see this example followed by others. Such a trend, at a time when our conventional forces are, in my opinion, only just adequate for the task allotted to them, would be little short of disastrous. If this situation were ever to arise, we should be wilfully jeopardising the enormous social and economic gains which have been made during the Alliance's lifetime. The close correlation between security on the one hand, and social and economic progress on the other, is still insufficiently recognised. It is, frankly, illogical to set social goals which undermine our conventional defense, for without security, these social goals would be entirely illusory.

Two further problems remain to be mentioned. First, we have recently entered a period in which there has been, on occasion, some serious disagreement among some of the Allied countries on a number of issues. This is probably due to an increasing interaction throughout the world of the interests of one state or group of states on those of others, and this phenomenon is by no means confined to Atlantic countries. Everywhere, trade, monetary and energy problems are demanding international solutions. While these solutions are being sought, there is liable to be disagreement.

But there is a second problem more special to the Alliance. This is the increasing tendency to consider Atlantic relations in terms of relations only between the United States and the countries of the European Community without regard to the rest of the allies, i.e. Canada, Iceland, Norway, Portugal, Greece, Turkey. This polarisation, if not checked, could be damaging. We, in Europe, must work for greater Atlantic unity. I have always been a strong "European" but I have never regarded European unity as something to be obtained in isolation, at the expense of our long-standing friends. I foresaw that an enlarged Community might complicate relations between Europe and North America but I had hoped that this would be offset, at least partly, by the increased role that a united Europe would be able to play. These hopes, however, have not yet been realised to any great extent; it has been the problems caused by increased rivalry that have been more in evidence, though there is no reason to believe that this situation will not change.

In my opinion, we should seek to return to the Atlantic concept of fifteen sovereign and equal members. We must consult within the Alliance between fifteen, and consultation must be sincere and timely, so that views can be considered and taken into account during the formulation of decisions. This is largely a matter of political will since the machinery is already there within our organization. I appreciate that there are often a number of barriers to consultation. Events can move fast, and there will always be failures due to human error. But if we quickly take steps to remedy the situation, when this occurs, little damage will have been caused. But what we must avoid is deliberate *faits-accomplis* by one ally or group of allies.

None of this is to say that the eight members of the European

Community who are also members of NATO should not attempt to reach agreement on subjects which impinge on the concerns of the Alliance. Indeed such discussions in the Community make a valuable contribution to consultation within the Alliance. But consultation elsewhere can never take the place of consultation in NATO because, if this were to happen, it would be Alliance solidarity that would suffer.

I make no apologies for having dwelt at some length on problems now confronting the Alliance, for it is only by facing up to them, and taking the necessary action, that we can look to the future with any confidence. It is essential that the Alliance continues to respond to the demands made upon it. There must be willingness to support the required defense spending by our governments; there must be a readiness by the European allies to maintain adequate conventional forces, along with a continuing commitment by the US administration to resist pressure for the withdrawal of American forces from Europe. Above all, there must be continuing solidarity between all the members of the Alliance.

If the Alliance is to continue to be an effective instrument for negotiating improved East-West relations, we will need, too, a good deal of realism so as not to be lulled into a false sense of security by agreements which have not yet stood the test of time. We must also maintain a sense of purpose.

The Atlantic Alliance has always been more than a banding together for defensive purposes. From the start, it was recognised that the democratic countries forming the Alliance shared common values such as freedom, democracy, individual liberty and the rule of law, which were coming under increasing attack from outside.

There is not the slightest doubt that we, in the West, have the necessary resources to ensure that, as long as it is needed, the Alliance can continue to provide for the security of ourselves and of our values and beliefs. But, under a democratic system, it is not enough for governments alone to appreciate the need for the Alliance, as such a policy, finally, depends on the authority and encouragement of public opinion.

That is why I so wholeheartedly welcome the decision to

publish the varied and constructive contributions. The discussion by responsible and knowledgeable authors of so many facets of the Atlantic relationship should contribute to spreading greater understanding of the Alliance and of its indispensable role in maintaining peace. For this reason, I am glad to help launch this book and wish it a wide readership.

1

Dangers We Must Face
by Michael Stewart

For twenty-five years the North Atlantic alliance has been a major fact in world politics. By its mere existence and power, and without the actual use of armed force, it has preserved the sovereign independence of its members, saving them from the fate of Czechoslovakia and East Germany.

Although it consists of one superpower, several medium, and several small powers, each has preserved its freedom of choice within the alliance, deciding how much or how little it would do in the common cause—a freedom which France has used extensively.

The security which it has engendered has enabled each member to keep military expenditure within bounds and, recently, has created the atmosphere in which it is possible to talk of better understanding with Eastern Europe. The alliance, and the four-power guarantee of West Berlin, have been essential conditions for the success of *Ostpolitik*.

Yet despite all this, harsh words have been hurled across the Atlantic in both directions and the alliance is under greater strain than it has ever been before. Historians will wonder at the frivolity of this exercise, conducted in disregard of the great issues involved: but they will get the picture wrong if they do not realize that there are solid—if, in the last resort, inadequate —reasons for the strain to which the alliance is now subjected. It is important that we should examine these reasons, and seek the policies through which the disputes can be resolved and the alliance preserved.

First, there is the feeling, bluntly voiced by President Nixon, that America is put to great expense, particularly in the maintenance of troops in Europe; that this is damaging to its balance of payments, and that its European allies should take account of this by being more generous in trade-bargaining with America instead of being so fully absorbed with the promotion of their mutual advantages in the development of European community policy.

There is a tendency in America to exaggerate this point; by far the greater part of the expense of conventional forces in Europe is borne by Europeans. America's trading anxieties are due at least as much to Japanese competition as to the policies of the EEC. Nonetheless, the point deserves more consideration than it has been given. Last year, conventional wisdom among Europeans was that, in transatlantic discussions, defense and trade must be kept separate.

This is totally unrealistic. They cannot be dealt with at one and the same conference; but the strain of defense on the American economy is real, and Europeans cannot approach trade discussions with America as if this strain did not exist.

There is the further possibility that difference over world monetary policy would provoke a similar EEC-U.S. conflict. But, whether for good or ill, monetary policy has not yet progressed so far, even within the EEC, as to make this a cause for immediate anxiety.

Next we must consider the fact that far and away the greatest share of the alliance's nuclear power is in American hands. This produces a double malaise in Europe. It produces among us Europeans an uneasy feeling of inferiority, and a dread that in the last resort our independence is in American hands.

This may seem strange to Americans, most of whom know quite well that if the Western European nations, for lack of the American nuclear guarantee, became satellites of the East, America itself would be in great peril, and the continuance of the "nuclear umbrella" is as much in America's interests as in ours.

But the feeling is real, and American policy should be aimed to dispel it. In particular, talk of removing American troops from Europe is likely to inflame this fear that the next step would be the disappearance of the nuclear guarantee.

The other part of the malaise arises from the knowledge that the United States and the Soviet Union alone are nuclear giants, and that, as such, they are engaged in the SALT discussions. Might they not be tempted to "do a deal"—as the phrase is—at the expense of their allies?

The moment one attempts to spell this out, its absurdity becomes apparent. Do we in Europe really believe that the United States, in return for nuclear concessions, would cease to interest itself in Western Europe, thereby so weakening its position in the world that it could never insure that any nuclear bargain was kept? And if this is not what we fear, then what is? Here again, America can help by continuing a policy of keeping its allies well-informed as to the progress of SALT.

Most recently, the alliance has been strained, in the context of the Middle East war, by the failure to reach a common policy on oil, energy or the Middle East itself. The cavalier treatment, by Europe, of American proposals to these ends was unwise—so was the American failure to consult, or even give adequate prior information of its nuclear alert at a critical stage in the conflict. Both these events suggest not so much ill-will as inadequate channels of communication. We have come to take the alliance too much for granted and neglected the need for close contacts.

Finally, there is what may be called the ideological strain. This affects public opinion rather than governments, but is not the less important for that. To many in Europe, looking at the American attitude to Greece and Spain, it appears that America does not greatly mind whether a country is a dictatorship or a democracy, provided it is not Communist.

It is doubtful whether the American government has yet taken the measure of this problem: but with the recent change of government in Britain it is likely to become increasingly important. An agreed policy of, at least, discouragement toward dictatorships may well be at least as desirable as an agreed energy policy.

Serious as these strains within the alliance are, they are not incurable. Already there have been some corrections of the hasty words spoken by both sides. The allies have only to remind themselves of the massive military preparations of the Warsaw Pact countries, and they will see their own differences in truer perspective.

America should then be able to realize how vital the continued presence of its troops in Europe is, and Europe can recognize that a helpful approach to the trade and balance of payments problem is something for which an ally can reasonably ask.

The processes of consultation can be improved and a more systematic effort can be made, through information services, to see that not only the governments, but the peoples, on each side of the Atlantic get a better understanding of how their partners think and feel.

In the long run, the ideological aspect will be the most important. We need to state more clearly what the purpose of the alliance is, and to make this message heard by the rising generation. An alliance solely for military defense has a negative inadequate appeal; it must be made clear, in words and deeds, that the search for détente and mutual force reductions is genuine, and that if it fails, this will not be NATO's fault.

An alliance solely against Communism is also too negative; it must be restated as an alliance for freedom, and for human welfare and justice.

Without this, the peoples of the West will not have the nerve or the will to continue the patient search for détente, or, meanwhile, to maintain their defenses.

As one of Bernard Shaw's characters expresses it, "The courage of faith will always outstay the courage of wrath." It is the faith that needs to be reasserted.

2

Strengthening Western Solidarity

by Pierre Harmel

If we look back over the last ten years, we see that during this decade all significant developments in international politics have been, for the countries of Western Europe, concentrated in three areas: the construction of Europe, relations with North America, and relations with the Eastern European countries.

On each of these fronts, the last ten years have been rich in events; strewn with difficulties, it is true, but characterized by continued effort. It has been, on the whole, a time of progress, a period of active European policy in three dimensions: coherent, dynamic and great.

The years from 1965 began badly, with the policy of the empty chair (France's withdrawal from EEC Council meetings); then the compromise of Luxembourg which made the community clumsy and substituted in fact the rule of unanimity in the Council of Ministers for that of the majority. But patience, determination and coherence enabled us, nevertheless, to do all that has been achieved.

I look back on this succession of days and sometimes seemingly endless nights, which did however bring, at dawn, a new achievement: the customs union, the beginning of the definitive period, dependence on our own resources, the successful negotiations with the four candidates for membership, the signature of the treaty of accession, its ratification by nine of the ten countries, the commencement of systematic political consultation and, at the Paris summit, the taking of political decisions which are to bring us, by 1980, to an economic and monetary union, and to a European union.

Thus governments and men, following others who had pursued the same policy during the preceding ten years, conceived and began to build an advancing Europe.

It was the same with relations with America. There too, in 1965, the decade started with problems: we were about to enter the twentieth year of the alliance, after which any member could leave it. A dark moment indeed, since in 1966 France ended her participation in the integrated peacetime military organization. But here also, within the union of the fifteen countries, a positive movement took place: all the member states decided to remain in the alliance, which was considered indispensable to security; a vigilant but not a static alliance, capable of adapting itself to changing circumstances, where political discussions about détente would have as much weight as decisions on defense; an alliance where, as we said even then, it seemed possible and more necessary than ever to define European obligations more exactly; the only venue for a balanced dialogue with the countries of North America.

Finally, the last ten years have led in a third direction: the Communist countries of Europe. Two themes have formed the background: regional, reciprocal, balanced and progressive disarmament in all the European countries; the search for conditions of peaceful co-existence between regions having opposing ideologies. There, too, difficulties and doubts were many. August 20 1968, in Prague, seemed to toll a knell. And yet, the treaty on the nonproliferation of atomic weapons was signed by more than eighty countries; the Vienna talks on balanced force reductions and the Helsinki conference on European security and cooperation started.

Why should we think back over these ten years, so creative in many ways, which up to a year ago appeared to show an irreversible advance toward European unity?

It seems to me that we should recall these years of effort in order to throw on the dark moments we are now experiencing light from the West, and thus to help and encourage those who now bear or will bear the responsibilities of the present.

Let us be frank: of all the months we have lived through in the past decade, the first three months of 1974 were the most negative and the most destructive.

The European community has met one defeat after another. To mention only the obvious: there is no regional policy, no fixing of farm prices, contradictory and competitive approaches to the problems of oil supplies, disagreement on a global energy policy, a breakdown in monetary agreements and thus a setback for economic union; in the same period, five government crises in three months in the nine countries of the community, and a very difficult approach to the European future for Mr Harold Wilson's government.

At the same time, the divergencies between the United States and the Europe of the Nine reached the stage of public quarrels, and the twenty-fifth anniversary of the Atlantic alliance, in April, took place in deplorable conditions.

And this at a time when we should be increasing our cohesion in order to be in a position to conduct negotiations with the Soviet Union and the Warsaw Pact countries in a context which from year to year becomes more difficult. It is true that eighty countries signed, more than five years ago, an agreement on the non-proliferation of atomic weapons, on condition that in exchange for the privilege of power thus granted to the United States and the Soviet Union these two countries should conclude between themselves agreements which would reduce the threat of intercontinental nuclear war. Instead, and in spite of the conclusion of the first SALT agreement, the opposite has happened, and in Europe the pressure of Soviet military power has become peripheral and naval, and has continued to increase. This is not the moment, therefore, to weaken the alliance nor to appear divided, at a time when negotiations are going on and when the granite of the Soviet attitude has no reason whatever to crumble.

Thus we are physically and morally surrounded, in Europe, by a series of cumulative dangers, both internal and external: precisely those we wished to guard against by unifying Europe and by a more open attitude to the East, neither of which is possible without the reinforcement and strengthening of Western solidarity.

How can we break the spell and resume our march forward?

I would like to indicate, from my close knowledge of the European community, the only place which has sufficient political power to take the action which should not be postponed, even for a few weeks.

The Council of Ministers must take the first step forward: the only project which will make this possible, and which will set in motion the others, is economic union, covering all aspects of the energy situation.

The nine countries together must overcome and correct by a suitable program the supply weaknesses which they have allowed to develop. An Arab-European conference may be useful, but can only deal with particular aspects of the crisis. The problem of the diversification of energy resources is enormous; Europe cannot solve it alone. But in order to take joint action with others, Europe must first define her own policy in this primordial matter. In order to treat with the old producers of petrol, and the new—British, Norwegian, Canadian, to speed up the study of all systems of power production, to revise our policy of commercialization and consumption of all forms of energy, a vast program is necessary, spread over a sufficient length of time.

A common will to face this obvious necessity would revive the dialogue which has become blocked on many other subjects.

Another matter is urgent: to restart the community machine we must call for the political intervention of the countries which successively have occupied the presidency of the Council of Ministers.

These countries, i.e. West Germany and France this year, not only know better than anyone why the community was founded, but their importance and their internal systems of organization allow the heads of their governments, with the help of their foreign ministers, to take adequate direct action. This personal and direct action has become essential.

Some marvel, others are surprised, at the imaginative, unifying and itinerant diplomacy of Henry Kissinger, in his efforts to solve the crisis in the Middle East. The difficulties in the community are, in their way, just as serious: before they become insoluble, I would suggest that the heads of government of the countries which, this year, preside over the council, and their foreign ministers, should also become, if necessary, pilgrims to the European capitals, until they have by their continued efforts restarted the community machine. There is no task more urgent and more essential.

As to the United States, only a strengthened community can reopen a fruitful dialogue and solve the problems between them.

But first, if I may suggest it, it would be advisable for everyone, on both sides of the Atlantic, to abstain from the anathemas which have been so freely and so uselessly exchanged in recent months.

Could we also refrain from arguing publicly about the respective roles of the United States and Europe in the world, and debates on bipolarism and multipolarism?

Could we not accept, more modestly, to treat our problems in the proper place; questions of security and détente in the Atlantic Council, and other concrete problems in the forums in which our countries meet, before discussing them on a global scale, as soon as possible, in a larger venue? So far as that is concerned, the simplest procedures will no doubt be the most effective: political exchanges between the United States and Europe do not need special institutions or systematic constructions.

But it is not conceivable that a situation should continue in which the President of the United States can meet regularly with heads of Soviet governments, and the European heads of governments have frequent meetings with the same Russian leaders, while similar meetings between the leaders of the European Community and those who govern America raise problems. If such meetings were to result in nothing more than what can be read in the final communiqués of certain Russo-European or Americo-Russian meetings, I think one might be justified in speaking of a second Prague Spring!

But we do not ask so much. For my part, I am in favor of the very simple system once suggested by Mr Robert Schaetzel, former U.S. ambassador to the community: "A delegation from the American government, led by the Secretary of State, should meet twice a year with the leaders of the Common Market. Such consultations are the more necessary since, all too often, each of the two partners is quite unaware of the problems of the other."

In our countries, hundreds of members of governments, members of parliaments, diplomats, civil servants, journalists, militants, Europe-builders, beginning with the commission of the Common Market and its staff, would be ready to support and promote a movement to avoid the dangers of disintegration, generating discord.

But few men have the political power necessary to redress the situation. They are named in the Treaty of Rome: they preside over the Council of Ministers, each in his turn.

It is to them that we must appeal, saying: If you take the initiative, if you set the example, if you remobilize all energies, if you explain the reason and the necessity for your undertaking to your allies, you will find, here and elsewhere, millions who are awaiting your lead. But do not delay, it is time!

Author's note: *The above article was written in March 1974, at the very height of the crisis. Let us hope that this was only a momentary depression in the course of European history. But even if events are now, some months later, developing in a rather less negative way, it is good to recall it to indicate the dangers inherent in a single moment's relaxation by Western leaders.*

3

Divergencies in
Basic Philosophies

by J. Robert Schaetzel

The notion of parallel if not common American-Western European interests has been an enduring and comforting assumption, central to the Atlantic relationship. The essential validity of the assumption seemed proven by the international economic rules and institutions born out of the post-war chaos—rules and institutions which contributed, in turn, to the unprecedented growth of world trade and prosperity. And conventional wisdom has had it that European and American life is dominated by a common commitment to democratic principles and political organization and to broadly compatible economic theories and values. A more recent common denominator, in the face of the economic furies of 1974, is that both sides of the Atlantic stand bewildered before similar and confounding problems.

Yet what seemed axiomatic so recently has now become subject to uneasy doubts. Examination of real or apparent divergencies between Europe and America may be useful, not to destroy the premise of common interests, but to re-evaluate and preserve this premise. Many of the differences are in the eye of the beholder. At a time of mutual questioning and suspicion, however, the insubstantial nature of the divergencies is less important than the attention and heat these divergencies attract.

Europe, for the moment, seems somewhat more inclined than the United States to resort instinctively to governmental intervention when confronted by internal or external problems. This arises in part from the natural momentum of continental governments socialistically inclined, with a general penchant for intervention; in part the difference is optical and semantic, magnified by America's nostalgic love affair with the free market society of its youth, accentuated by Nixon's predilection for, if not the execution of, policies to this end. Without value judgment and with considerable caution, the basically different American and European political-economic philosophies can lead to varying policies. For example, Germany and the European Commission press for worker participation in corporate management—a program widely at variance with American practice. European governments and unions (though the latter may be weak by American standards) place severe restrictions on the freedom of management to hire and fire its employees. The allocation of resources to welfare programs in Europe takes a far larger slice of the European national product than is the case in the United States.

Current events have highlighted another basic difference: the relative abundance of agricultural products and raw materials in the United States as contrasted with Europe. Europe's absolute and irremediable dependence on imported fuel has thus led to a different strategy toward the Arabs—to barter deals, to nascent industrial aid programs and to military sales arrangements. As a result of this disparity of resources between Europe and America, with the latter a major exporter of farm products and the former working toward autarchy, there is no natural common agreement on international agricultural trade. This difference was dramatized in the curious but heated maneuvers preliminary to the next round of trade negotiations.

The European Community initially insisted that agriculture be negotiated separately from the industrial sector; the United States took the contrary view.

There has been a clear and possibly growing cleavage between America and Europe on "globalism" versus "regionalism." The community's contentious association arrangements with Mediterranean, African and some Commonwealth countries, and the free trade area with the northern neutrals, suggest Europe's regional bias. America's political, security and economic interests move it irresistibly toward global solutions.

A clear divergency is developing in the approach, if not in the basic interests, of Europe and the United States toward the developing countries. European aid—as measured by percentages of gross national products—is well above American performance, but Europe also shows a concern disconcertingly less evident today in the United States. The enlargement of these differences could have ominous consequences. For instance, Europe, seeking favors and markets, could well expand its preferential association arrangements, which would provoke new conflicts with America.

Europe has been philosophically attracted to the technique of commodity agreements as a device for dealing with surpluses; the United States, in recent years, has been dogmatically and doctrinally opposed to such pacts. The inversion of the world raw material supply-and-demand situation, with shortages not surpluses the major question, might drain this issue of its past bitterness. If Washington were to be more pragmatic and relaxed, and let the international bargaining process demonstrate the difficulty, even impossibility, of working out these arrangements, the issue might then disappear.

Viewed dispassionately, and within the full panorama of our troubled world, these differences between America and Europe seem small and manageable. The monetary system with its floating rates, the absence of competitive devaluations and the cooperation of treasuries and central banks to absorb mushrooming oil revenues suggest that major economic problems can be handled sensibly. Yet Atlantic economic affairs can easily get out of hand in the adversary climate that some on both sides of the Atlantic appear intent on generating. An atmosphere of mutual suspicion, of issues maneuvered to achieve domestic political advantage, of aggressive pre-negotiation of problems, hinders the quiet resolution of economic issues. For example, for over a year Europe and the United States have inched toward a new round of major trade negotiations. The Atlantic consensus on which successful negotiations must rest was hardly sturdy, but it becomes dangerously fragile in a world whose economic problems are entirely novel and poorly understood.

A further disruptive element is European shock at finding its painfully gained economic equality with the United States in 1973 suddenly washed away by the energy-financial crisis. Thrown back into a position of general (political, defense and economic) subordination, Europe becomes easy prey to diverse propaganda suggesting that the goal of American policy is dominance and perpetual hegemony. A companion risk is that America will be carried away by its newly recovered economic strength *vis-à-vis* Europe and will find irresistible the temptation to throw this weight about. Nixon's blunt threats in Chicago on March 15—which tied America's defense role in Europe to unspecified concessions on economic matters—was a sign of submission to this temptation.

It is a situation laden with irony. Affluent and interdependent, America and Europe also confront similar, complex problems that neither understands. Is full employment possible without excessive inflation? Can we cope intelligently with a world in which raw-material problems suddenly transmute from surplus to shortage? Is there a solution, or even a tentative answer, to the dilemma of the poor countries, which labor under exploding populations and high import bills and which face not theoretical but actual famine? Can the economic system digest the surplus $50 billion the oil-producing states will accumulate in 1974?

Our common history and deep-seated, inherited interests all suggest that the economic divergencies between Europe and America could be submerged in a new quest for the constructive solutions. But the Atlantic nations have drifted onto a contrary course: to suspect rather than to trust; to aggravate rather than to placate; to dramatize issues rather than to control them. The positive notion of "community," whether within Europe or between Europe and the United States, is lost in an orgy of nationalistic excess. If the Atlantic countries continue down this path, there is no question of their capacity to destroy not only themselves, the Atlantic relationship, but the defenseless, resource-poor Third World as well.

4

Politics and the Money System
by Antonio Giolitti

Utopia and Reality: this could well be a fitting title for the international monetary system from Bretton Woods to our own day.

We can now state with hindsight that the system could perhaps have been conceived with a modicum of prudent pessimism: the international monetary system drawn up at Bretton Woods postulated an international political system quite different from that based on the power relationships which were stabilized in the postwar period and which still persist. The balance of rights and obligations in the monetary field, on which the Bretton Woods system was founded, presupposed a similiar balance of power and dove-tailing of attitudes in the political field, that is to say an international pluralistic and not an imperialistic order.

Let us briefly recall the cardinal points which acted as a framework in this system of balancing reciprocal rights and obligations:

The duty of each state to contain the swing of exchange within restricted limits above and below fixed parities; the

c

duty of debtors to convert into gold or into the currency of creditors the amounts that the latter might happen to have in debtor currency; the right of debtors to procure creditor currencies from the International Monetary Fund within stabilized limits; the rights and obligations bound up with the acquisition and sale of gold in accordance with the relationship between the official price and the market price.

Particularly in respect of the fundamental right and obligation of convertibility, the balance of the monetary system depended on the symmetrical balance of the political system. With regard to the right and obligation of convertibility, each individual state had to be placed and recognized in conditions of parity with any and every other state, independently of its geo-political dimension or of its ranking as a power.

The right of creditors to insist on conversion and the obligation of debtors to satisfy such demands had to be equally applicable to all. The monetary system plunged into crisis when this equality was canceled out by the political system.

In August 1971, the United States officially declared the suspension of the dollar's convertibility into gold, following on the circumstances that for some time this convertibility had in fact been restricted or made null and void because of political considerations, and, as a result, any request for converting accumulated dollars into gold came to be interpreted as a hostile act directed against the United States. It can nevertheless be said that the crisis of the Bretton Woods international monetary system is a reflection of the crisis in the international political system in the West, and that the future of the former is bound up with the future of the latter.

An analogous and parallel crisis has also hit the Western European sub-system within the framework of this system. The crisis is even graver in this context: for it is a crisis of identity, a crisis touching the very heart of existence. Confronted by what has been called "dollar imperialism" the European

Economic Community has vanished. The true scandal lies not in the so-called imperialism, but in the vanishing trick.

There is nothing scandalous or surprising in the fact that the United States, a superpower enjoying hegemony in the West, should attempt to solve the monetary crisis by obtaining from the rest of the world—to quote Gordon Tether in the Financial Times—"an appropriately respectful and indulgent attitude towards dollar imperialism."

The problem is accordingly, and before all else, a European one, and it seems to me that it may be expressed in these terms: a system of fixed rates of exchange postulates convertibility; the United States has clearly stated that dollar convertibility is totally excluded; a regime of floating and uncontrolled exchange is incompatible with European economic and monetary union; accordingly, the only way of eliminating these contradictions is not to reduce oneself to a position of "wait and see" in respect of what the Americans will do or will impose, but to control and reduce fluctuations in European currencies, and to erect the bases of a European regional monetary area so as to organize a common fluctuation against the dollar.

Such a solution is coherent with the prospective policy of a balance of power between great regional areas, and it is a prospect which seems to me more realistic and acceptable insofar as it negates the idea of an Atlantic Community, in which Europe would be destined to lose for good and all its own identity and to remain a shuttlecock between the clash and encounter of the superpowers.

The creation of a monetary area certainly postulates the will and the method to harmonize the different structures and economic infrastructures within the confines of the European Community. The main difficulty to be overcome in order to achieve this harmonization lies in the varying distances that different countries have to traverse before they reach the level of full employment, and so achieve a distribution of the national product which is socially acceptable.

If this is the difficulty to be overcome, it is necessary to take care not to put the cart before the horse; it is not feasible to seek first to impose a rigidly fixed parity of exchange or an immediate common currency and then only afterward to undertake those policies which are consistent with achieving full employment and the balance between different regions. On the contrary, regional policy comes first, and with it comes the possibility for national governments to promote social justice for their own regions and citizens within the context of a community system.

Both at the level of the European Community and at the level of the West as a whole, monetary balance depends on political balance, and this in turn depends on the ability to translate in terms of institutions and attitudes the values of liberty and social justice which determine the rule of a democratic society.

The oil crisis together with the grave impact that this is exercising on the international monetary system both make the building of a new international order even more necessary and urgent. Will the West be able to do this? Its future depends on it. Moreover, the experience of the oil crisis has confirmed that the building of such a new order can in no way be based on the supremacy of a superpower.

Admittedly, the immediate effect of the present crisis has been to reinforce the hegemony of the dollar and to sap Europe's strength. But the combined effort of the United States of America and the as yet disunited states of Europe should tend to overcome this imbalanced situation. The West must rapidly clear its own internal crisis if it is to assume its indispensable role at a global level.

The urgent task facing the West—and on this depends its future—is to put right the catastrophic imbalance which has come about between those underdeveloped countries which produce oil and those which do not; for it behooves the West (the United States and Europe) to insure that the international monetary system functions in such a way that the increase in the balance of payments gap of oil-importing countries is made to favor underdeveloped countries.

Such countries should be placed in a position where they can increase their imports from industrialized countries by making use of a part of the new monetary base allocated to them. With the remaining part they would be enabled to tackle the major burdens imposed on them by oil imports. The industrialized countries would tackle the major burden of oil imports either by increasing the availability of the monetary base or by increasing the flow of exports to the underdeveloped countries. In this way the oil crisis could prove to be the historic opportunity which induced the West to become the promoter of a new international order, both political and monetary, based on parity of rights and obligations, and on solidarity and justice.

5

Proposals for Achieving a New Economic Policy

by Henry H. Fowler

I would hope that this book, coming as it does on the heels of the recent public confrontation between the U.S. President and his Secretary of State and the leaders of most governments of Western Europe, would serve to let some steam out of the boiler rather than build up pressure. I feel it may also give us an opportunity to assess calmly the problems of the Atlantic community, and, hopefully, to surface some practical proposals for their solution, or at least their alleviation.

It is not important whether the proposals or solution bear a "Made in U.S.A." label or have their origins in Europe. They will not be effective unless they are designed to serve, not just a given national or regional interest, but the common interests of the Atlantic nations and the cause of peace and prosperity throughout the world.

What are some of the elements that contribute to this Atlantic crisis? First, we are moving into an era of seeming détente, where the issues of international trade, finance and investment loom much larger and more divisive than they were in the black-and-white era of the cold war.

The United States and other democratic nations find it more difficult or less necessary to maintain the strength and unity needed to assure the momentum toward a meaningful détente which we earnestly seek but which is not yet a reality.

Second, the shift in the relative economic positions of the United States, Western Europe and Japan has not yet been reflected in an alteration of respective responsibilities or an acceptance on all sides of shared responsibility for the maintenance and development of a world economic order. Leadership by the United States may be too often confused with unilateral action. And international economic drives of the European Community and Japan seem all too often to reflect parochial self-interest or inward-looking motivations.

Third, the increasing interdependence in economic and financial affairs, while yielding unprecedented material benefits, limits the ability of the nation-state to manage effectively its own affairs free from and without taking into account external impacts and forces.

Fourth, the institutions and practices that governed the economic relationships of the Atlantic nations—and, indeed, the Free World since World War II—the Bretton Woods system, the GATT, the OECD, are outmoded or inadequate in their structure and power to deal with the highly integrated international economy that has emerged. There is the resultant peril of a reversion to a pattern of Atlantic relationships marked by unilateralism, excessive nationalism, neoisolationism, or inward-looking public conduct that characterized the prewar era.

It is an ironic twist that many of the factors that contribute to the present crisis result from the successes of Atlantic cooperation in the last twenty-five years in producing peace and prosperity in that area.

The success of NATO has led to a phase of security which depends upon continued strength and unity. The success of the international trade and payments arrangements since World War II has vastly increased trade, capital movements and the movements of people across national borders, particularly in Western Europe, North America and Japan. International financial and security markets now influence developments in national financial markets. Inflation and recession, unlike infectious diseases, cannot be screened out at the customs post. Businesses increasingly look beyond national boundaries for markets and investments. Multinational companies with direct and portfolio investment move in both ways across the North Atlantic, leading to a declining national orientation of corporate behaviour, at least in the Atlantic countries.

In essence, there is the fact of interdependence in the Atlantic area not only with each other but with the Third World. If it is fragmented into several separate and potentially unfriendly and uncooperative blocs, common disaster or threats to peace and prosperity will surely emerge.

But whatever the answers—however competently organized and skilfully designed—they will not be effective without one essential accompaniment. That is the renewed dedication of the peoples and political leaders of the Atlantic nations to the continued development of an open community of nations. This community must be committed to the systematic and orderly utilization of international economic policy geared to the practice of international cooperation for the common good through well manned international institutions, public and private.

This continued development must involve, far more than we have yet witnessed, a willingness to pool national sovereignty in limited and precisely defined areas of economic decision making, and/or the undertaking to follow codes of international conduct in limited and defined areas of governmental activity. Through this practice of international cooperation, comity, and supranational action we can achieve goals beyond the reach of a single nation to accomplish alone.

The increasing interdependence of the nations and economies and peoples of Western Europe, North America and Japan is an important basis for an evolving and advancing economic order of this character. Their shared values, similar patterns of political and economic organization and conduct, and common economic objectives are sufficiently compatible to ground a high degree of consultation and collaboration. The institutionalization of this cooperation by the Atlantic nations in trade, monetary affairs, financing and capital movements, international investment and development, tourism, energy affairs and general economic policy can be the nucleus of a larger, worldwide international economic system just as an outward-looking European Community can contribute more than the nations of Europe operating separately.

This then is the year when the conjunction of various international events is likely to determine the future of international economic policy for some years and decades to come.

This is the year in which it will be determined whether one in Europe can be a good Europeanist and a good Atlanticist at the same time.

This is also the year in which it will be determined whether an American can be a good American and a good Atlanticist at the same time.

There is no choice between a European Europe and an American Europe. The only choice is an Atlantic Europe working with an Atlantic America.

One truth is abundantly clear. The security of Western Europe and North America is indivisible; it has proved to be so in the past and will remain so for the indefinite future. That being so, the withdrawal of American conventional military forces from Europe in this nuclear age would be an irreparable and irreversible event, destructive of the equilibrium of forces in that part of the world which has been the foundation of peace and prosperity and the basis for a movement toward détente.

Let no political leader on either side of the Atlantic lose sight of that fundamental fact.

Acts of political will at the highest level on both sides of the Atlantic will also be necessary in recasting the economic and financial relationships to convert our existing practices and institutions for international consultation and cooperation into effective instruments capable of the formulation and execution of constructive international economic policy.

In this task, we should not be rivals but allies.

The future of an initiative of this nature depends on responsible and far-sighted leadership in the free democratic societies willing to lead.

It also depends upon an educated citizenry willing to support or, on occasion, to stimulate national leadership to establish and operate increasingly effective instruments for international economic cooperation.

6

Too Much Independence in Atlantic Oil Bargaining?
by J. E. Hartshorn

In the American energy scenario that Dr Henry Kissinger presented to his Washington energy conference in February, there were two, or perhaps three, main elements. The first was that the USA was ready to lead Europe and Japan—indeed, Dr Kissinger wanted to lead all oil-importing countries—into consultations with the Organisation of the Petroleum Exporting Countries to seek some new pattern, interdependent and mutually advantageous, for the world oil trade.

The second—a concomitant of this—was that all other importing countries ought immediately to stop seeking bilateral deals with the OPEC countries to arrange their own long-term oil supplies for the future.

The third element of the same energy scenario, however, was that the United States intended to put itself into a position, as soon as may be, to cease being an oil importer at all.

Dr Kissinger and the Administration's then energy advisers saw nothing contradictory about this. Nevertheless, even within the first six months after that Washington conference, a marked reassessment of priorities in American policy towards international oil supply had become apparent. Any urgency there was in the preparations for a collective bargaining approach to OPEC seemed to have evaporated—on the American side. (Not on the European. Nor, it would seem, among at least one or two OPEC governments either. But Dr Kissinger had been engaged—more productively and no doubt more interestingly —elsewhere.) Secondly, having looked more coldbloodedly at "Project Independence", American energy advisers seemed to be backpedalling.

Thirdly, this summer the USA has concluded with Saudi Arabia a far-reaching agreement on arms supply and other "economic cooperation", and has talked of offering some other OPEC governments the same kind of deal. There have been some official attempts to pretend that this bilateral deal does not affect oil. But it is being followed by new arrangements between Saudi Arabia and Aramco, the American oil concessionnaires there, which will outpass and effectively "trump" the sixty per cent participation deals made in other Gulf OPEC countries earlier this year. Long-term guarantees of supply to these US companies—and potentially to the USA, if it wants the oil imports after all—appear to be involved here. And the American Government's protestations have not persuaded its European and Japanese allies that this is anything but the biggest bilateral oil deal of all time.

No Western oil-importing government is guiltless of hypocrisy here (except France, which has gone on with bilateral oil deals and no apologies). All the others, even while echoing Dr Kissinger's condemnations of bilateral sin, have gone on quietly with whatever deals of this kind they already had in train or in preparation. Nor was much pained surprise, even, in order about the American double-think on oil. Many of these governments had always suspected that at one of the levels of American energy policymaking (and there are a bewildering number of levels) an American-Saudi "special relationship" had been in the making ever since Sheikh Yamani first proposed it in autumn 1972.

On Europe's side, commitments and now preliminary approaches to an "EEC-Arab" dialogue have begun. Dr Kissinger's objections to this appear to have been mollified by vague promises of consultation and rather firmer assurances that this dialogue will not be allowed to interfere with (a) his further Middle East peace-making diplomacy or (b) any concerted oil importer-exporter bargaining, if and when this is revived as a practical proposition.

Moreover, unexpectedly, the EEC sent its first joint official message ever to OPEC's Quito conference in July. It sought to head off an increase in tax rates by arguing that the international oil companies' high 1974 profits were illusory, or at any rate fleeting. Dr Kissinger is said to have been asked, but to have declined, to join in this *démarche*. (Japan's reaction was the same.) In fact, proposals to increase OPEC tax rates were deferred. Nor was any increase decreed in tax reference prices for oil. But it would be unrealistic to imagine that the EEC's approach had anything to do with this. Once again, oil importers owed their respite to Saudi Arabia's compunction about prices that it considered too high. And if any Western voices were influencing that Saudi attitude, they seemed more likely to be those of Dr Kissinger and President Nixon.

Some detailed studies and discussions did follow upon the Washington energy conference, in the so-called Energy Co-Ordinating Group; these were completed by the late summer. The twelve governments involved worked over a number of issues such as energy conservation; joint energy research and development; oil import and supply sharing in case of emergency; and "the role of the oil companies". These same twelve governments had long been accustomed to discussing most of this same subject-matter within existing institutions, notably the OECD—where France and other developed importing countries can join in. By the end of this first "ECG" exercise in July, agreement had been reached on a supply-sharing formula backed by the USA—on condition that responsibility for this and some of the other issues would largely pass back to the OECD.

So only limited practical coordination of oil-importing governments' energy policies has been achieved since that Washington conference—so far. But the independent policies that the main importers have pursued have not in practice collided too much, or cut right across each other. It is in the economic sphere bordering on the oil trade, and today hugely affected by it, that lack of coordination really is hurting, and is endangering the world economy.

This again, is a sphere where the OECD and IMF are, or ought to be, effective. So far in 1974, they have not been. The essential problem, now familiar but still extraordinary, is the huge trade surplus OPEC countries are running because they cannot collectively spend on current goods and services the whole paper value they get for their oil at today's prices. The mirror-image of this, for all oil importers or for OECD again considered collectively, is an equal and opposite huge trade deficit. Since the one is unavoidable, so is the other.

All OECD governments are aware of this. All, too, pay lip-service to its consequence, that exaggerated efforts by any one oil-importing country to maintain or improve its former trade balance can only succeed by beggaring one or other of its neighbours. The more a few oil importers—Germany, the USA, perhaps Japan—succeed in redressing their oil trade balance, the deeper into deficit they will force other weaker oil-importing economies such as Italy, Britain, perhaps France.

But in spite of their lip-service, most of the main oil-importing economies, strong and weak, are in fact doing just what they agreed to be collectively unwise—seeking to balance their oil trading accounts, primarily by deflationary policies at home. (The rampant inflation they are trying to check with these policies, unfortunately, is also nearly as strong as ever.) Whether deflation all round—except in a few countries such as Britain, whom their OECD partners dismiss as economically feckless anyway—will tip the world into depression this winter is still uncertain. But the OECD governments' reaction to the oil payments crisis—rather than the oil crisis itself—is making this danger more real than at any time since the war.

Belatedly, some hopeful signs are now appearing of adjustment in the world's financial mechanisms to handle at least the "technical" problem of OPEC surpluses. Some OPEC governments are beginning to "lend longer", and invest the funds they cannot use at home in a wider range of productive opportunities abroad. Many OECD governments are toying with special medium-term bond issues guaranteed against currency devaluation, essentially tailored to the OPEC lender. In one way or another, these surpluses are returning to world financial centres, enabling the "recycling" needed to finance the (developed) world's oil imports. (But too little, from the West or the Middle East, seems yet to be in train to help the developing countries that have to import oil too.)

Even if the accelerated urgencies of 1974 are in some way muddled through, this oil problem will not go away. Each OECD importer sighs for an escape from its import dependence on OPEC. The USA is now reexamining its first heady commitment to seek complete energy independence. But it has to bear in mind that this option is in any case not open to most other large oil importers. Two or three other lucky ones—the Netherlands, Australia, soon Britain—can also achieve self-sufficiency in energy. The rest—notably most of Europe and Japan—cannot avoid heavy continuing dependence on imported oil and gas. The countries' immediate energy situations parallel those of the United States. But it clearly does have the resources at home to fuel, eventually, all its own needs—at a high cost, but one that current trends in oil import prices just might make bearable. Most of its partners in "Atlantic-Japanese energy" simply haven't the energy for this.

Project Independence, taken at face value, postulated reducing US imports straight away; obviating any need for them by 1980; and making the USA a potential net exporter of energy by 1985. This probably won't happen. But very considerable economies in imports probably will. Even to start with, American imports are only about sixteen per cent of its total energy use. This spring, not to be outdone, the EEC produced its own revised projections, seeking to bring the share of imported energy down from about sixty-two per cent now to twenty-five per cent by 1985. This hope seemed at least as far-fetched as the original US ideas of complete energy self-sufficiency; perhaps more so. Japan displayed fewer illusions. Its revisions imply no more than a reduction of oil import dependence from seventy-five per cent to about seventy per cent. So this current identity of interest as oil importers could theoretically soon narrow, perhaps towards vanishing point.

Even if America in fact seeks much less than its full "Project Independence", some of the other importers hope that this would puncture oil prices in a world market from which the USA, once again, would have opted out. If so, the USA might maroon itself on an island of relatively high-cost—though safer—indigenous energy production. Europe and Japan would be left largely dependent on imported oil that would inevitably be less secure—but might again become cheaper, too. That was what happened last time America chose to insulate itself from the world oil market, throughout the sixties. (Perhaps not, or not only, because it did; but *post hoc*, anyway.) So some American analysts fear that once again American import-phobia could help confer cheaper energy on its industrialized competitors.

Whether such a replay of the sixties would actually happen, even at some higher general level of prices, is rather debatable. OPEC won't necessarily expand its export capacity to cover more import demand than can realistically be foreseen. Moreover some of its members, such as Saudi Arabia, have a formidable flexibility in their potential output, downward as well as upward—and are certainly under no pressure to maximize their oil revenues, most of which for years ahead can accumulate only on paper. So precisely what effect a degree of American energy independence, and perhaps some US withdrawal from oil importing, might have on prices is no easier to prophesy with confidence than anything else about the oil business nowadays.

In European capitals as well as Washington, experts are now examining the likely costs of reducing oil import dependence.

The direct costs will be hard enough to reckon. But there are indirect, perhaps hidden costs too, in these import-saving exercises. The direct investment cost of the local energy that a country develops will be obvious, if not easy to measure in advance. But the greater self-sufficiency in energy these governments hope for would not come simply from a build-up of local energy. They also postulate a slowdown of growth in national energy demand.

Even though we can expect some improvement in the efficiency of energy use, that will probably mean a slowdown in these economies' general economic growth too. Indeed, the extra national growth forgone could be a much bigger cost to an oil-importing economy than the extra investment in local energy. And both, incidentally, represent real resources, diverted or sacrificed. We must remember that until such times as all OPEC countries can absorb all their rocketing revenues in real resources within their economies, this will not be fully true of oil importing. Today, and for quite a number of years ahead, part of oil's import "costs" to the industrialized West will simply accumulate as their claims and our promises of future payment in goods and services. In the meantime, these surpluses will involve no transfer of real resources at all.

But while there are hidden costs to self-sufficiency in energy, these may also offer some hidden flexibility for oil bargaining. Advanced economies do not sacrifice real growth cheerfully. If through discussion with OPEC they could see a chance of more dependable supplies and more predictable prices— preferably somewhat lower—for imported oil, there is a large margin of flexibility in their plans for import-saving. And even if they developed most of the local energy they have in mind, they need not forgo as much economic growth.

The interests of even the industrialised oil importers are not automatically identical, and may later diverge more widely. But the exporters' interest, as demonstrated inside OPEC at Quito, aren't automatically identical either. Consultations at various working levels between OECD and OPEC, probably, can be put together fairly soon. In such arguments, the economic and political bargaining strength will be oddly distributed. But each side has considerable latitude; and neither has blocked too many options for the other in advance. These remain necessary—though not sufficient—conditions for effective bargaining.

7

The Responsibility of Multinational Firms

by Emilio G. Collado

There is increasing concern about the role of multinational corporations in the world economy, and particularly about their influence on the national economic, social, and cultural fabric of the countries in which they operate.

National governments are considering how best to "control" the large multinational enterprises and many countries have introduced a variety of restrictions governing these companies' activities. At the international level, a major UN study of the broad impact of multinational corporations on economic development and international relations has just been completed. Its major recommendation is to establish a permanent UN Commission which would provide for a continuing dialogue among governments, multinational corporations, labor groups, and other interests on issues relating to the multinational corporation.

The Organization for Economic Development and Co-operation, whose membership consists of industrialized countries only, has also embarked on a broad-scale study of the multinational corporation. The Business and Industry Advisory

Committee (BIAC) to the OECD, representing the business community from OECD countries, is in touch with OECD concerning the various aspects of the study. BIAC will cooperate with OECD as this study progresses, by providing its advice and assistance, where appropriate. Hopefully, the UN and OECD efforts will increase public understanding of the role of multinational corporations and promote a better climate in which multinational corporations and governments can work cooperatively toward the achievement of their respective goals.

Clearly, a major aspect in assessing the behavior of multinational corporations is how they view their responsibilities to society. Generally, multinational corporations see their most important responsibility as conducting their particular business well—by producing a high-quality product or service efficiently and offering it at a reasonable price. A second level of responsibility is to ensure that the indirect impact of business operations is consistent with national goals—for example, with respect to protecting the physical environment, reducing social inequities, and improving labor skills. A third level of responsibility concerns efforts to enhance the broader social environment in countries in which the corporation has operations, for example, by providing support for programs in health and education, community development, and national cultural activities. Multinational corporations generally accept these three levels of responsibility not simply because it is "the right thing to do," but to a great extent because such behavior promotes successful long-term operations in foreign host countries.

Since no multinational corporation has unlimited resources, it must choose carefully among the many investment opportunities which arise. In making long-term investments abroad, multinational corporations are vitally concerned that the basic "rules of the game" affecting these investments will remain relatively stable, or at least predictable, over time.

Although conflicts with governments have not been common,

the potential for conflicts in the goals of multinational corporations and governments is a cause for serious concern, particularly among host countries. This concern reflects a number of factors. For example, the large size of many multinational corporations has been cited as evidence of power over national economies. However, most of the wealth of multinational corporations consists of fixed assets, which cannot be summoned to bring pressure to bear on either individual currencies or governments.

The many examples of unilateral government actions—imposed production and export quotas, price controls, enforced sell-outs, and in some cases expropriations—and the accommodations made by multinational corporations, do not indicate that global size entails substantial power. The success of multinational corporations in operating in many countries over long periods largely reflects their ability to adapt to—not escape from—the national requirements and goals of individual host countries, while continuing to carry on effective business operations.

There are a number of positive actions which both corporations and governments could take to reduce, if not eliminate, potential sources of conflict. First, to the extent that tax policies may distort international investment decisions, such distortions should be reduced. This suggests further intergovernmental efforts to achieve the following: eliminate discriminatory tax treatment of foreign investment by host countries; prevent international double taxation (where multinational subsidiaries are fully taxed by both host and home country governments); and bring about greater harmonization of national tax policies.

Second, it has been alleged that multinational corporations are able substantially to reduce their total tax burdens by adjusting the prices charged for goods and services transferred among their various affiliated companies. The extent of distortions in this area has been greatly exaggerated. In general, multinational corporations follow normal commercial practices in their interaffiliate transactions, and prices charged realistically reflect the market values of the goods or services transferred.

"Manipulation" of transfer prices is usually neither feasible nor desirable, for a variety of reasons. Moreover, the penalties for using improper transfer prices are severe. When a government decides such prices are inappropriate, the unilateral imposition of tax liabilities results in double taxation for the multinational corporation.

It is clear that multinational corporations ought consistently to reflect arm's-length or market prices in their interaffiliate transactions. (In fact, current U.S. law requires U.S.-based multinationals to do this.) On the part of governments, it would be most desirable to reach international agreement that arm's-length or market prices for interaffiliate transactions be used to determine taxable income, and thereby avoid unilateral government decisions to tax income which has already been taxed by another government.

More generally, multinational corporations might agree on a voluntary "code of conduct" describing broad principles of acceptable behavior in various areas. This would undoubtedly contribute to a better climate of understanding for the corporations generally. Such an investors' code could broadly support positive adaptations to the host country's social and economic goals, and condemn certain undesirable forms of behavior. The International Chamber of Commerce has made a useful contribution to developing such principles for behavior.

Concerning government policies, full international coordination or harmonization of national policies affecting multinational corporations is probably not feasible, and in some cases not desirable, for individual countries. However, there are some policy areas in which greater coordination is possible, and would result in substantial benefits to multinational corporations and governments.

Beyond the area of tax policy, greater international coordination of national policies toward foreign investment would also be useful. However, regional harmonization of host-country policies for the purpose of substantially restricting the activities of foreign investors may backfire, if the adverse business climate causes multinational corporations to undertake alternative investments outside of such regions.

On the other hand, multinational corporations would be significantly encouraged to undertake new investments in developing nations if they had a greater assurance that their operations in these countries would not be subjected to substantial new forms of discrimination or controls once their facilities had been constructed.

Thus, a measure of international agreement on some maximum extent of discrimination or restrictions affecting foreign investment in various policy areas—such as taxation and foreign exchange remittance policies, for example—could substantially reduce the investment risks perceived by multinational corporations. As the discussion continues among investors and governments, elements of a broad inter-governmental agreement could evolve and be available for individual governments to endorse voluntarily.

An intergovernmental agreement could also include a broad commitment by host governments to submit foreign investment disputes to the international conciliation and arbitration facilities of the World Bank or ICC. Such a commitment would dramatically improve the climate for investment in these countries, and would avoid some of the "confrontations" which have characterized past investment disputes.

8

Multinationals and their Impact on the U.S.A.

by Lane Kirkland

The AFL-CIO, the trade union center of the United States, has been calling attention, for many years, to the growing problems posed by the radical changes in international economic relationships of the past twenty-five years, particularly of the past dozen years. One of these changes has been the mushrooming spread of multinational corporations and banks, with worldwide operations and international transfers of finished goods, components, technology and funds.

Multinational companies operate globally—with plants, sales agencies and other facilities in as many as forty or more countries. In addition, they have license, patent and joint-venture arrangements with other companies in various countries. They manipulate the location of their production and sales internationally, depending on such factors as taxes, labor costs and foreign exchange rates. They can juggle exports, imports, prices, dividends and currencies from one country to another, within the structure of the corporation and for the advantage of the corporation.

Most multinational companies are U.S.-based. But there are

major English, French, Japanese, West German, Italian, etc.,
multinational firms. In addition, agencies of some of the
Communist countries have been operating enterprises in other
nations and also have developed joint ventures with multinational corporations, such as the Fiat venture in the Soviet
Union.

These developments have substantially changed the nature of
world trade and international financial relations. However,
theories of world trade are still rooted in the much different
world of the eighteenth and nineteenth centuries and serve to
confuse policy issues concerning the realities of the 1970s.

A substantial portion of what national governments report as
imports and exports is actually intracorporate transactions
among the subsidiaries, plants, sales agencies and similar
divisions of the multinational firms. Another substantial portion
of such reported imports and exports is between the multinational firm and other companies, in various countries, with
which it has license, patent and joint-venture arrangements.

The spread of multinational corporations, particularly those
based in the United States, has resulted in the internationaliza-
tion of technology. One of the underlying reasons for the inter-
nationalization of American technology has been U.S.
government encouragement of American companies to export
technology.

The very existence of multinational firms and banks, with
their ability to rapidly move large amounts of funds from one
country and/or currency to another—aside from the possibility
of deliberate speculation in currencies—is an ever present
potential threat to relatively stable currency and exchange-rate
relations among nations.

A decision that may be rational for a multinational firm may
have adverse effects for workers or consumers or social progress
in the multinational's home-base nation or in other nations. Or
what may be a rational decision for the multinational company
or bank may create severe difficulties in international monetary
relationships. Yet there is no international law, regulation,

supervision or accountability of multinational firms and banks.

The AFL-CIO has naturally focused its attention on the impact of U.S.-based multinationals on U.S. workers and the U.S. economy and society.

Sharply rising investments by U.S. firms in foreign operations have exported U.S. jobs, technology and production facilities. These investment outlays soared from $3.8 billion in 1960 to an estimated $16.3 billion in 1973.

In a paper prepared for the Joint Economic Committee of the U.S. Congress, Prof. Peggy B. Musgrave of Northeastern University stated that "sales of [U.S.] manufacturing subsidiaries abroad are now two to three times the level of U.S. exports of manufactured products. It should be recognized that the economic and political effects of maintaining a share of foreign markets via foreign production are very different from doing so via domestic production and exports. The principal difference lies in the effects on labor productivity and shares in national income. Foreign investment may enhance the private profitability of U.S. capital but it is likely to reduce the real wage to U.S. labor as well as the government's tax share in the profits."

Prof. Musgrave's conclusion may be put in a more general context: the operations of multinationals, including their technology-transfers, may enhance their sales and profitability, but they are likely to reduce the real wage of workers in the home-base country. In addition, they may distort economic and social development, with adverse impacts in the host countries.

The substantial changes in the world economy, including the rapid spread of multinational firms, have had a devastating impact on the position of the United States in international economic relationships. This deterioration has eroded America's industrial base, with increasingly serious adverse impacts on U.S. workers, communities, industry and the national economy. Major segments of American industry, including sophisticated production, have been hit hard by these developments. The unregulated operations of the multinationals are a major factor in causing these adverse impacts.

The shutdown of manufacturing operations in the United States resulting from such transfer of technology and capital depress the American economy by the export of hundreds of thousands of jobs, the loss of payrolls, the loss of national tax revenues, the loss of local purchasing power, the loss of local taxes and the "ripple out" effect on local services. Hard-hit communities face empty factories, slackened business on Main Street, unemployed workers and an eroded tax base.

The energy crisis underscores the problems posed by the unregulated operations of the huge multinational oil companies. These operations, which have been aided by lavish U.S. tax concessions, have been a substantial factor in making the United States, a major oil-producing nation, increasingly dependent on imported crude oil and petroleum products, transported in foreign-flag tankers. The major U.S. oil companies placed growing emphasis, in recent years, on foreign investment in refining, as well as in exploration, drilling and crude-oil production and in foreign-flag shipping.

This growing dependence on imports made the United States vulnerable to the Arab bloc's blackmail in mid-October 1973. Moreover, the major companies—those based in the United States as well as in foreign countries—have acted as agents and tax collectors for the Arab oil-producing areas. Exxon, the U.S.-based multinational giant, even broke its agreement to provide oil to the American fleet in the Mediterranean Sea, at the demand of Saudi Arabia.

The giant oil company multinationals produce crude oil, refine it into heating oil, fuels, lubricants, and materials for the petro-chemical industry, as well as gasoline. They produce, refine, distribute, ship, and even retail their products in an integrated process, in a large number of different countries. They are joined together in joint ventures and interlocking relationships. The U.S. companies' fleets of huge tanker ships fly foreign flags to avoid U.S. registration, regulation and American wages.

The five U.S. giants—Exxon, Texaco, Mobil, Gulf and Standard Oil of California—plus Royal Dutch Shell and

British Petroleum are known as "the seven sisters." These are the huge multinational firms that dominate the world's production, distribution and retailing of oil and petroleum products, through their own operations and various joint ventures. Moreover, the oil giants are also conglomerates—for example, they own large percentages of U.S. natural gas, coal and uranium reserves and pipelines, as well as ventures outside of the energy area.

The companies have passed on to consumers the staggering increases in royalties charged by the oil-producing nations—royalties which the multinationals subtract from their tax liabilities to the U.S. government. Moreover, they took advantage of these conditions to boost their prices sharply on their substantial U.S. production. The result has been huge price increases for American consumers, tremendous increases in oil company profits and lost revenues to the U.S. government.

As a result of the trend toward nationalization of crude oil production in many of the key oil-producing areas, the integrated multinational oil company giants are shifting the point of their major profit-making from crude oil to refining, shipping, distribution and retailing. Their success, in this shift, is indicated by the sharp increases in their cash-flow during the period of the Arab bloc's reduction of crude oil output and embargo.

The adverse impacts of the deterioration of the U.S. position in international economic relations and the impacts of multinationals are much tougher and more direct on workers and on consumers, generally, than on capital or top-management officials. Capital is mobile. Investments can be moved out of an unprofitable business to other companies, industries and countries. Top-management officials are usually much more mobile than workers.

In contrast, workers have great stakes in their jobs and their communities—skills that are related to the job or industry, seniority and seniority-related benefits, investment in a home, a stake in the neighbourhood schools and church. There are also significant adverse impacts on the collective bargaining strength of affected unions, on the wages and labor standards of workers in adversely affected industries.

In addition, as the energy crisis shows, there are adverse impacts on the price level, and on consumer buying power.

Ideally, major parts of the solution to the growing problems posed by the multinationals probably are in the international arena, through international regulation of trade and investment. But there isn't even an international organization, at present, to develop and implement regulation of the operations of the multinationals. Moreover, there is no international law on the operations of multinationals, even for the protection of the multinationals, which have their own variety of problems. The needed international regulation of multinationals is still to be achieved.

However, workers cannot be expected to continue to sit by and await such needed international action. In the absence of international law, international regulation, or even international machinery affecting multinational firms and banks, nations have acted and will continue to act to regulate the operations of multinational firms. In the United States, it is the view of the AFL-CIO that U.S. government action is urgently needed for the regulation, accountability and proper taxation of U.S.-based multinational corporations and banks.

As we in the AFL-CIO see it, there is urgent need for an adequate U.S. trade and investment policy—for the orderly expansion of trade, including the prevention of growing adverse impacts on American workers and communities, for effective measures to regulate the operations of multinational companies; for curbs on runaway plant developments; for elimination of U.S. tax and other concessions that subsidize the foreign operations of U.S.-based multinationals; for fair and effective taxation of multinationals; for regulations and curbs on the export of American capital and technology.

9

Measuring the Outcome of the Mideast Crisis
by Bernard Lewis

The Arabs and the Israelis have fought their fourth full-scale war, and both have emerged with some gain in military credit. It may even be that they will succeed in reconciling their conflicting rights and achieve the peace that both so badly need.

The United States and the Soviet Union have stood by their protegés and helped them to the best of their differing abilities. The Americans in particular have shown that, even in the midst of a desperate domestic crisis, the government is capable of swift and resolute action in an emergency. The trauma of Vietnam is passing, and once again the awesome might of the United States is clear for all to see.

It is just as well, for the performance of Western Europe in this crisis can give little ground for either pride or hope. Much has been said about the British and French arms embargoes, but these are only a part, and by no means the worst, of a general European reaction.

All of Europe with—if the Arabs are right—only one exception, has supported the Arab cause; some enthusiastically, some half-heartedly, some sanctimoniously, some apologetically, but all to the same effect and all, so we are led to believe, with the same lack of real conviction. This is called evenhandedness, and its result has been to arouse the mistrust of Israel, the contempt of the Arabs, the appetite of Russia and the anger of the United States.

The dilemma is often presented as a conflict between sympathy and interest—sympathy for Israel and interest with the Arabs. But it is by no means as simple as that. Sympathies are sharply and genuinely divided, and emotional support for either side can distort the perception of national interest. Nor is the definition of national interest as evident as is suggested. European interest in Arab oil is obvious, and it might seem reasonable to assume that an effort to gain Arab goodwill would insure the flow of oil at commercial prices. But what is reasonable is not necessarily true.

An oil embargo is a powerful but blunt weapon. And the Arab producers knew that their use of it, if maintained, would cause inconvenience in America, hardship in Europe, and suffering in Asia and Africa. Nevertheless, they appeared to be willing to inflict this hardship and suffering on their sympathizers, in order to secure the dubious advantage of inconveniencing their presumed adversaries.

But oil is not the only or even the major problem, nor are the rights and wrongs of the Arab-Israel conflict itself. Transcending these is the larger question of the global confrontation of the free West and the Soviet East, which has continued in various forms and under various names since 1945. The latest name for the balance of terror is détente. The rise of Israel, it has been argued with some color of justification, provided the opportunity for the Soviet intrusion in the Arab lands—though it may be noted that they did quite well in South and Southeast Asia, and for a while in Africa, without such adventitious aids.

But the scene has changed, and today, for better or worse, Israel is the rear bastion against Soviet domination of the Middle East and North Africa, protecting, by a strange paradox, the independence of some of the Arab states themselves. Israel, whatever its intentions, could never really menace the independence of the Arabs or the integrity of their civilization. Russia could turn them into another Uzbekistan.

The only true victory that either the Arabs or Israelis could achieve is a peace which would free them from the need to call upon the superpowers for help. The recent war demonstrated to both sides the extent and the perils of their dependence on such help.

The position of the two super-powers is fundamentally asymmetrical. America is far from the Middle East, and has limited interests in the area, mostly commercial and defensive. The Soviet Union is near, and has older and vaster ambitions. Israel's fear is that America will desert it; Egypt's fear is that the Soviet Union will embrace it—a fear that continues despite improving U.S.-Egyptian relations and President Anwar Sadat's criticism of the Soviet role in the October war.

The front line against the Russian advance is still held, as for centuries past, by Turkey and Iran, and it is no doubt for this reason that both countries have been the targets of a great effort of organized subversion. In Turkey, radical "youth movements" for a while brought the country to the verge of chaos; in Iran, the regime has been subjected to a worldwide campaign of vilification by radical and self-styled "progressive" elements, who combine their dislike of the Shah and support for other autocrats with the approved international alignment and the correct ideological tincture.

Both countries remain basically pro-Western, but both, because of a well-grounded mistrust of the effectiveness and reliability of the Western alliance, have found it wise to improve their relations with the Soviet Union. With a Soviet-dominated Levant, both would be open to greatly increased pressures from front and rear, and might well be neutralized or enveloped in the great Soviet march to the Mediterranean, the Red Sea, and the Indian Ocean, so important in the growing struggle with China. Symptoms of this process may already be discerned in the level of Soviet official activities in both countries, and in the measure of acquiescence they have won for Soviet needs and requirements.

There is some dispute about the Russian role in the launching of the October offensive. The Russians certainly knew that it was coming and could have stopped it or, as required by the détente agreements, have given warning. They did neither, but on the contrary fanned and spread the flames until a change of wind suddenly transformed them from arsonists to firemen. Had the attack succeeded, the Soviets, not the Arabs, would have been the victors, with incalculable consequences for the whole world, and perhaps the permanent subjection of the Arabs to a new and greater empire.

Israel, without having desired or sought the role, is the barrier on this path. The Soviet Union knows it, and that is why it continues to support and encourage its unrewarding allies; President Nixon knows it, and that is why he—of all American presidents the least sentimental—was willing to risk Arab wrath by going to Israel's aid. For the same reasons, which of course have no bearing on the merits of the Arab and Israeli cases, America might have expected the cooperation of Western Europe. But America did not receive the cooperation of Western Europe, which preferred to leave this problem, too, to its ally across the ocean.

How much easier to follow policies and make statements directed to short-term needs, in the confident belief that the Americans alone would incur the odium of doing what had to be done, and thereby save not only Israel, but also Europe and ultimately the Arabs themselves from the dangers that menaced them.

In the short run, the oil weapon brought the Arabs great diplomatic victories. In the longer run, it did their cause little good. The main victims were countries already sympathetic to the Arabs; short supplies and long prices will not have increased their sympathy. The Americans were only marginally affected, and even derived some advantage, reflected in the rise of the dollar. American industry gained from the weakening of its more vulnerable competitors in Europe and Japan. More important, America was given the opportunity to halt the current trend in the direction of greater dependence on imported oil, and thus avert the dangers which this would otherwise have brought.

The real gainers were the non-Arab oil producers, who enjoyed a windfall, and the Soviet Union, which rejoiced, especially in its Arabic broadcasts, in the division of Europe and the disarray of the Western alliance. These events will inevitably encourage those not unimportant groups in the United States who feel that Europe is not worth defending, and that America should reduce or terminate its commitment. If their views prevail, then the Soviet Union will have won a great victory—a catastrophe for Europe and ultimately also for America.

It is fashionable to use the word "Finlandization" to describe the Soviet program for the future of Western Europe. The term is an undeserved compliment to some of the governments of Europe and an undeserved insult to Finland. The Finns, isolated and friendless, have preserved a large measure of both freedom and independence because they showed that they had the courage and determination to defend themselves against any odds, and the Russians know it. Can one say the same of Europe?

10

Implications of the
Yom Kippur War

by Eugene V. Rostow

For all the risks of hypothetical history, it is reasonable to contend that World War II would not have occurred if Britain had agreed with France to use force, if necessary, to prevent the militarization of the Rhineland in 1935. But in the middle 1930s, Britain could not break the spell of somnambulism which kept it from perceiving the danger, and acting to deal with it.

The October war in the Middle East raises the same kind of questions for the Atlantic allies, for China, and for Japan. All are agreed in opposing Soviet hegemony either in Europe or in Asia. Soviet domination of the Eurasian land mass would transform the world balance of power, and, therefore, threaten the territorial integrity and political independence of each of these nations, and of many more as well. But European and American public opinion, lulled by the soothing rhetoric of détente used by nearly all the allied governments, is only dimly aware of the nature of recent events and of their implications.

At the moment, the West has too few political leaders in the spirit of Churchill and Truman, of Adenaur, De Gasperi, Acheson, Attlee, Schuman, and Monnet—men who trusted their people and were willing to offer them nothing but blood, sweat and tears. Détente with the Soviet Union—an agreement of peaceful coexistence, based on respect for the Charter of the United Nations with regard to the use and threat of force in international relations—is a political condition the allies have sought through thick and thin since 1945, and even before that. It must always be a major goal of Western policy.

As the October war and its aftermath demonstrate, however, this goal has not been reached. The Soviet role in the war was fundamental and deliberate. It cannot be reconciled with the Charter of the United Nations and the decisions of the Security Council, nor with the promises Leonid Brezhnev made to President Nixon in the ill-fated détente agreement of May 29 1972.

In May 1972, Mr Brezhnev publicly assured the United States not only that the Soviet Union would generally abide by the rules of "peaceful coexistence", but that it would exert all its influence to achieve a diplomatic settlement of the Arab-Israeli conflict in accordance with Security Council Resolution 242 of November 22 1967. That resolution was sponsored by the British government, and supported by a concerted Atlantic diplomacy achieved through consultations in which all the allies, including France, participated fully. Resolution 242 calls on the parties to reach an agreement of peace, pursuant to which Israel would withdraw from territories it occupied in the course of the Six-Day War to secure and recognized boundaries established by the agreement of peace. Because Egypt had violated the agreement with Israel negotiated on its behalf by the United States in 1957, Resolution 242 requires no Israeli withdrawals from the cease-fire lines until the parties concur in an overall agreement of peace, establishing security arrangements including demilitarized zones; guarantees of maritime rights through all the international waterways of the region; and a just settlement of the refugee problem. This is the essence of the famous "package-deal" of Resolution 242, which had—and hopefully still has—the support of all the Atlantic allies, and of many other nations as well. In 1967, Soviet representatives said of Resolution 242 that it was the first time in the history of the cold war that they used the phrase "package deal" in a positive sense.

Far from persuading Egypt and Syria to enter into the negotiations called for by Resolution 242, however, the Soviet Union spent six years, billions of dollars and the time of many thousands of its experts in training, equipping and organizing the Arab armies for the attack of October 6 1973. Even though Egypt's President Anwar Sadat cleared Soviet troops out of Egypt in 1972, many Soviet military men participated in the war, not as front-line troops, but as operators of highly sophisticated military technology and as planners. The Soviet Union gave the war its full diplomatic support and even urged distant Arab states to enter the fray. The Soviet Union refused even to discuss a cease-fire until it was clear that Israel had won the war.

The Soviet plan was to exploit Arab hostility to the existence of Israel as the detonator of a war which would produce irreversible change in the area and thus make the Arab states completely dependent on Soviet protection. It is not difficult to imagine the moral shock to Western opinion if the war had resulted in the destruction of Israel.

The October war could not have taken place without Soviet backing, which offered Arab leaders the irresistible appeal of undoing what they regarded as the injustice of the long chain of events flowing from the Balfour Declaration. It was the most serious and fundamental Soviet thrust of the entire postwar period against the Atlantic Alliance—a bold and carefully prepared attempt to neutralize Europe, dismantle NATO, and drive the United States out of the Mediterranean and Europe itself. If the great arc from Morocco to Iran were brought under Soviet control, the allied forces arrayed in Europe would be outflanked and in peril. With the oil and space of the region in Soviet hands, the fate of Europe, the Russians thought, would be settled. What was at stake in the October war was therefore infinitely more serious than the possible outcome of earlier cold war confrontations over secondary issues like Iran, Greece, Turkey, Berlin or Cuba. The October war was not a tactical but a strategic move, aimed at the heart of the alliance.

The October war should therefore be perceived as a Pearl Harbor, a flash of lightning revealing the nature of Soviet policy in all its grimness. It dramatized a threat to the security of the allies which can only be met if they act together with the greatest possible energy, imagination and urgency. They have a little time in which to concert their policy, thanks to the victory of Israeli arms, backed by the staunch diplomacy of the United States, with the assistance of Portugal and, less visibly, of others among the allies.

But this brief allowance of time will do the allies no good if it is not used.

Are the allies rallying in harmony to meet the common danger? Or are they treating the October war as Britain treated the occupation of the Rhineland in 1935?

This is the concern behind the American government's vigorous recent efforts to persuade the allies to develop concerted Atlantic policies on a long list of fundamental problems which affect their security and prosperity as directly, and as vitally, as the possibility of invasion by land across the central front in Germany.

Since Suez, the allies have often differed on a number of political, security and economic questions not directly affecting the central front. The United States is now convinced that the comfortable pattern of intermittent allied dissonance which has prevailed since Suez is no longer tenable as a basis for policy.

In this, the American government is clearly right. The rising level of Soviet pressure makes that pattern a luxury we can no longer afford.

This is not a time for mutual recriminations about the many mistakes and missed opportunities of the last twenty-five years.

Each of the allies has made mistakes, many of them serious, all of them painful. It is a psychological reality that each of these blunders left behind a residue of resentment which affects the politics of the alliance.

But the allies are bound together by other and more positive memories. They worked together successfully to build NATO, restore Europe and develop a far-reaching and progressive Western economy, on which their own prosperity, and that of many other nations, depends. They should approach the issues of the day in the spirit of that set of memories, and with full awareness of the fact—and it is a fact which no one can alter—that they share an indivisible destiny, which can be protected only if they work together.

In the nuclear age, the security of Europe requires the permanent cooperation of the United States and its European allies. None of the economic problems of the industrialized world can be dealt with except through the cooperation of the OECD members, and a number of other nations, including the oil producers and other developing nations. The degree of integration of the OECD economy means that the main economic problems of the worldwide Western economy are now beyond the reach of any nation or group of nations acting alone, no matter how powerful.

Different combinations of nations are required to deal with the main political problems of the world—those which are universal, like the control of nuclear weapons; and those which are regional, like the security of Europe, Asia, Africa and Latin America.

One of the most urgent of these political issues is the enforcement of the Security Council's binding decision of October 22 1973, that the parties to the Middle Eastern conflict must negotiate a just and durable peace, in accordance with Resolution 242. The October 22 Resolution is the most constructive single step ever taken by the international community in the conflict over Israel's right to exist. The chances of fulfilling the mandate of that Resolution would be enhanced if the process of carrying out the Security Council's decision is backed by the concerted influence of the Atlantic allies, which was decisive in achieving Resolution 242 in 1967.

Peace between Israel and its neighbors will not alone assure the interests of the alliance in the Middle East. But no program for safeguarding those interests can succeed unless the Security Council decision of October 22 1973 is obeyed.

The nature of Soviet foreign policy and the implacable problem of nuclear deterrence have rendered many ideas obsolete. In 1949 many people, both in Europe and in America, thought that, once Europe was unified, American forces could be withdrawn. Europe could then take over its own defense and participate in world affairs as a strong and independent polity, well disposed to the United States and Canada, to be sure, but an autonomous third force between the Soviet Union and the United States nonetheless. The idea was just as attractive in the United States as it was in Europe, for it seemed to offer the United States an opportunity to withdraw from dangerous entanglements in foreign quarrels, and return to a stance far more congenial to the notions America has inherited about the rightful role of the nation in world politics. This nostalgic yearning for America's isolated past is the powerful force behind the proposals of Senator Mike Mansfield and others to withdraw American conventional forces from Europe and the Mediterranean.

Neither American isolationism nor the concept of a third-force Europe has a legitimate place in the world of 1974. The security of Europe requires the indefinite presence of American forces in and near Europe, to make sure that nuclear deterrence remains credible, and that in a limited crisis the allied governments would not face the choice between abandoning a vital interest and using the nuclear weapon. The degree of integration of the European and North American economies reinforces this principle. If there is to be any hope of curing the cancer of inflation, and maintaining a reasonable rate of economic growth, the Atlantic economy must be managed as a unit, by methods of cooperation which would have seemed utopian only five years ago.

But men cling tenaciously to the ideas of their past. The isolationist impulse is still strong in the United States. And in Europe some still contend that Europe must choose between the principle of a "European Europe", and that of an "American Europe". There is no such choice. For reasons rooted in the nature of things, there can be no Europe except an Atlantic Europe, just as there can be no America except an Atlantic America. On that footing, and only on that footing, both Europe and America can retain their separate and altogether authentic personalities.

If the October war and its consequences do not convince European and American opinion that Atlantic solidarity is the rock on which their future must be built, we have lost our instinct for political reality.

11

U.S., Europe and Russia

by Leonard Schapiro

One can speak of the United States and the Soviet Union as the two nuclear superpowers. But what of that vague entity, Europe, of which, in geographical terms, much of the Soviet Union and the Soviet empire of people's democracies form a part? One can think of Europe in one sense as a group of states which share much of their history and tradition, and which, in contrast to the Soviet Union, are linked to the United States by common ancestry and a democratic way of life. But what does one then do about the awkward cases of Spain, and until recently Portugal and Greece, vital for the Atlantic defense system, but remote from democratic practice? Or about some of the waspishly neutral Scandinavian countries? The idea of Europe has always been an amalgam of contradictions. For our present purposes it might be best to confine ourselves to the European members of NATO and forget that some of them have not been too convincing advocates of the defense of man's freedom that NATO stands for.

It is plain that economically, Europe can rival both the superpowers. Militarily, for a long time to come, its defense will continue to depend ultimately on the nuclear might of the United States and on U.S. troops and conventional arms as well. One would have to be very naive indeed, in view of what has happened in recent months, to believe that there is no longer any need for vigilant defense against the Soviet Union.

The strategic arms limitation agreement has merely saved the Soviet Union vast capital which the United States could have invested without crippling itself, while a comparable investment on the Soviet side would have crippled the Soviet Union. The agreement has, in any case, been virtually nullified by rapid (and unforeseen) Soviet technological advances.

The louder the clamor for peace issuing from the Soviet side, the greater the preponderance which the Soviet Union has built on NATO's flank, while the ringing phrases on cooperation for peace have been worn rather thin by Soviet policy over the Middle East war, which the Soviet Union made possible and which it now seems to be doing its best, to keep going as long as possible.

In such a situation of danger, what is more essential for the survival of the "free world" than Western European unity and close cooperation between Europe and the United States—if only to stop the Soviet Union from exploiting U.S. isolationism and anti-American feelings among the European powers in order to weaken NATO. This obvious policy, if the freedom of the Western powers is not to be endangered, or extinguished, is not going to come about overnight.

On the European side there is, probably as the product of wishful thinking and successful Communist propaganda, disbelief in the Soviet danger, in contrast to the situation which united Western Europe at the end of the forties. Then again, there is a lack of confidence in the purity of U.S. intentions and a suspicion (fostered by Soviet political warfare) that the United States and the Soviet Union intend to settle the troubles of those tiresome smaller states between themselves.

There is also a not unjustified fear of American economic

imperialism. And there is a strong sense in Western Europe that we, unlike the Americans, are immediately in the firing line and that if the Americans contribute, even disproportionately, to the defense of that firing line, that is, after all, not a matter of the United States doing Europe a kindness but of saving its own skin.

There is equally genuine resentment on the U.S. side. The trauma left by Vietnam does not make it easy for Americans to live with the notion of their troops still serving overseas in what, all too readily, comes to be looked at as a foreign concern. There is force in the argument that if the United States bears so large a share of the military burden of NATO, it has a right to expect some economic benefits from its European partners—even if the petulant rudeness of President Nixon and Henry Kissinger was not calculated to make the argument more acceptable to Europeans.

The famous doctrine of "containment" was perhaps pusillanimous in the pre-nuclear Soviet era when "liberation" might have succeeded. But it is certainly vital for our safety now. This calls for a sense and imagination all around in rebuilding unity between Western Europe and the United States. If the Europeans must learn to work more closely with the United States, the U.S. government must learn to be more imaginative in its relations with the European powers.

For example, it is futile to expect that the European powers will necessarily and immediately fall into line with U.S. policy in the Middle East when these European powers are to an immensely greater degree dependent for economic survival for some time to come on Arab oil.

But if the Europeans must shed some illusions, so must the Americans. The fruits of the so-called "détente" policy should surely have taught the U.S. administration by now that it is erroneous to suppose that sweetness and light have descended on the Kremlin since Mr Nixon's visit to Moscow; or that there is some special relationship that the United States can develop with the Soviet Union—unless it be the special arrangement that Polyphemus promised Odysseus, to be devoured last.

F

Above all, Mr Kissinger and Mr Nixon must really stop propagating the view that what they call "détente" is the only alternative to a nuclear conflagration. This is nonsense. All the experience of U.S.-Soviet relations since 1962 proves that avoidance of nuclear conflict is the cardinal principle of Soviet policy; it has nothing whatever to do with the complicated and ingenious exercise in political warfare which the Soviet leaders were clever enough to sell to the Americans under the label of "détente" ten years after 1962.

But there must also be considerable rethinking on both the American and European sides of the whole of their trading and financing policy toward the Soviet Union. Are they really wise, for example, to bolster the Soviet military effort by selling Russia the equivalent of three years' research and development, as one computer firm recently boasted it had done? The matter is complicated both in the United States and in Western Europe by the fact that much of Western trade with the Soviet Union is in private hands, as witness the U.S. grain deal. But the interests of private dealers are not necessarily the interests of the United States or Britain.

If the Western powers are to hold their own against Soviet totalitarian foreign policy (which, of course, includes trade) they will have to reconsider the degree of freedom which independent traders should be allowed. Above all, the Western powers should never forget to exploit their strengths against the Soviet Union. If the Soviet Union needs credits or technology as badly as it appears to, then it should pay a political price for them. But such a policy can only be pursued successfully if there is unity of action between the United States and Europe and among the Western European powers, since in default of unity the Soviet Union will play one power off against the other.

The Soviet leaders must learn that their "détente" gambit, with its potential economic prizes, must be paid for; and, above all, that vapid phrases about peace and friendship which are so dear to the Soviet leaders (and not entirely displeasing to Western statesmen anxious to improve their political reputa-

tions) are no substitute for real political changes and concessions. It is only if such changes take place that it will be
possible to speak of détente in any real sense of the word.
Meanwhile, in the words of Chairman Mao, the best advice for
the United States and for Europe is: "When the fox is friendly,
double the bolts on the door of the chicken coop."

12

China, USSR, and the West
by Leopold Labedz

The Chinese attitude towards Europe and the U.S.A. is certainly not "an enigma wrapped in mystery". It is determined by three rather obvious elements of the present geopolitical situation: the Soviet threat, the weakness of Europe, the lowered profile of the American foreign policy after Vietnam.

During the last decade the Sino-Soviet hostility continued to deepen and the Soviet Union came to be regarded in China as "enemy number one". As both antagonists made abundantly clear, this fundamental fact underlies the Chinese foreign policy posture and it explains why American and European conciliatory gestures towards Moscow are viewed with suspicion in Peking.

The Chinese attitude towards détente is basically determined by the Sino-Soviet conflict.

When after the Cultural Revolution China emerged from self-imposed isolation and entered the mainstream of international political life on the level of state relations, it was the result of its perception of the growing Soviet menace. It was this factor which necessitated a shift in Chinese foreign policy.

This brought about restoration of diplomatic relations with those countries which had recognized China before the Cultural Revolution, efforts to win recognition from other countries, entry to the United Nations and *rapprochement* with the United States. The Soviet invasion of Czechoslovakia and the Brezhnev Doctrine made China even more acutely sensitive about the danger of Soviet expansionism.

The shift in Chinese foreign policy has as its primary motive the reduction of this danger. This led not only to a new policy towards the United States and Japan, but also to the support of the idea of a strong, united Western Europe which would continue to tie down Soviet military forces and provide a political counterbalance to the Soviet Union on its Western flank. Hence the Chinese criticism of the Soviet *détente* moves in Europe (*Peking Review,* February 8 1974):

"The Soviet Union . . . while making further military deployments in Eastern Europe, took pains to press for the heads of the European governments to meet before the end of last year in the third stage of the conference on European security and cooperation, so as to lay what it called a 'solid foundation' for European security and cooperation. It hoped in this way not only to consolidate its overlordship in Eastern Europe, but also to lull the vigilance of the West European countries, divide them and edge the United States out so that it could now pull the whole of Europe under its sole domination. . . . The Soviet leading clique has tried its best to advertise 'relaxation' of the international situation. However, the reality of the stepped-up Soviet arms expansion and war preparations in Europe and its intensified contention with the United States in the Middle East have relentlessly exploded the détente myth . . . ."

While remaining conscious of the Soviet threat, the Chinese line has shifted from stressing the peril of a Soviet pre-emptive military strike against China to emphasizing that Western Europe is the Soviet primary target, that the USSR is "feinting to the East in preparation for an attack on the West".

Although the Chinese have an obvious interest in saying this, it does not necessarily make it invalid. Soviet expansionism is indeed likely to be channelled where the prizes are higher and the risks are lower. The opportunities in Europe are not seen by the Soviet Union as military (contrary to what Chinese propaganda implies): the aim here is a slow and gradual increase in Soviet political influence. In this process military preponderance (even if it falls short of nuclear blackmail) is seen by the Soviet leaders as being of utmost importance.

Strategically the outflanking of Europe can come either through the Balkans and the Middle East or more indirectly through a Soviet "drive to the South" towards the Persian Gulf. The latter is of particular interest to China as it involves the threat to Pakistan and the Soviet presence in the Indian Ocean. This is seen in Peking as part of the Soviet strategy of encirclement of China, in which Afghanistan and India are to play an important role.

The Soviet press countered this by accusing the Chinese leaders of "giving their silent approval to the growing U.S. military presence in the Indian Ocean" (*Krasnaya Zvezda*, June 9 1974), and of "justifying the American military presence in Asia" (*Izvestiya*, July 14 1974).

The aim of the Chinese warnings to Western Europe is, according to Moscow, "to urge the militarist circles in Western Europe to step up the arms race, strengthen the aggressive NATO bloc and return Europe to the times of the cold war. . . . Although Peking declares that Europe has become 'the battlefield of the two superpowers', every effort is directed towards frightening West European countries with the 'Soviet threat' " (*Pravda*, June 6 1974).

While the Chinese assert that for all their talks about détente the two superpowers are engaged in a struggle to achieve world hegemony, the Soviet press maintains that the Chinese have "modified their foreign policy at the 10th (Party) Congress [held in 1973] in such a way as to be able to use various forces, including the imperialist circles, for their struggle with the Soviet Union, the paramount obstacle on the way to Peking's hegemony" (*Mezhdunarodnaya Zhizn*, January 1974). In their interpretation of the Cultural Revolution the Soviet analysis points out that this shift had occurred at the plenary meeting of the Central Committee of the CCP in Lushan in Summer 1970:

"During this meeting the substance of the secret talks between Peking and Washington, which had been for some time conducted on the instructions of Mao Tse-tung and Chou En-lai, were first disclosed. Everything points to the fact that other Chinese leaders, including Lin Piao, were unaware of this. . . . Mao's new line contradicted the resolutions of the 9th Party Congress. In his speech at this Congress Lin Piao . . . referred to the 'latest Mao directive' about the 'new historical period—the period of simultaneous struggle with the U.S.A. and the Soviet Union'. Now Mao proclaimed a completely 'new stage', a stage of collaboration with the American imperialism, to conduct a struggle with the Soviet Union. This new turn proved to be too sharp even for such an old hand as Lin Piao." (*Voprosy Istorii*, December 1973.)

There can be little doubt that during the Cultural Revolution there were important differences of attitude among the Chinese leaders about the problems of foreign policy, and that some of these differences persisted after it was over. But it is extremely doubtful that any Chinese leader could afford (or was inclined to take) a pro-Soviet line: the differences were about strategy and tactics.

There is also little doubt that the American-Soviet efforts towards détente were seen with growing distaste, if not alarm, by Peking and that the new internal struggle which erupted after the 10th Congress, although it is basically concerned with internal affairs, may well get entangled with the issues of foreign policy. It is not just a question of struggle for succession, but also of the basic future orientation of China which is involved in the esoteric formulations of the attacks on Confucius and Lin Piao, Beethoven and Antonioni. Whatever the symbolic status of the "sick horse" sold by the Chinling production brigade to the Taoyuan production brigade in the opera *Three Ascents of Peach Mountain*, one can be quite certain that Mao's successors will have to face the same dilemmas as he does, and that their margin of manoeuver in foreign policy will also be limited. Given its geo-political context and the nature of the Sino-Soviet conflict, China can either have a policy of equidistance *vis-à-vis* the Soviet Union and the U.S.A., or a policy of *rapprochement* with the U.S.A. (with the Soviet Union as "enemy number one"). Sino-Soviet *rapprochement*, the usual bugbear of Western analysts, is unlikely in the present state of Sino-Soviet relations and even in the post-Maoist period, although factional struggle can be seen as offering an opportunity which will eventually be exploited by the Soviet Union.

It is not however likely that Soviet hopes in this respect will materialize. None of the contending groups aspiring for power in post-Maoist China is going to improve its chances of success by a visible "Soviet connection". The conflict with the USSR is too fundamental to make this anything but a political "kiss of death". Only in a situation of extreme desperation (i.e. to save itself) would a faction envisage such a course and even then it is difficult to imagine what the Soviet Union could do, short of direct military intervention, to help. Such a course in the future would, however, raise for the USSR the same types of risks as a preventive war would today. The reasoning which postulated either Soviet preventive war against China or a Sino-Soviet reconciliation proved wrong in the past and it is possible that it would prove wrong in the future. Neither-war-nor-peace between Russia and China is a likely prospect in the post-Maoist situation as well. The best that the Soviet Union can hope for is that China will fall back into a state of internecine warring and thereby knock itself out of the international game.

At present, however, such a prospect is fairly remote. None of the warring factions (or groupings) show any particular pro-Soviet inclinations and it is particularly ill-advised to correlate such an attitude with either "moderation" or "radicalism" in the Chinese political spectrum. As Michael Oksenburg and Steven Goldstein pointed out (in *Problems of Communism*, March-April 1974), it is in any case misleading to apply to these groupings the labels of "right" and "left".

Whatever the usefulness of such terms in the Western context (and it is declining even here) they are particularly confusing when applied to the Chinese political scene.

The patriotic motive, whether rooted in the Chinese cultural tradition or in national communism, practically excludes any permanent solution of the Sino-Soviet differences. The chasm is too deep and this limits the possible post-Maoist alternatives not only from the point of view of possible foreign policies, but also of the attitudes taken towards them by the contenders for power. It is also unlikely that the struggle for succession after Mao's death will be so bitter and so prolonged that it will bring about the disintegration of a centrally unified Chinese state on the mainland, of a return to the "warlord period". If this perspective is not likely the Soviet chances of a successful China policy are very small indeed.

But whatever the future of Sino-Soviet relations, their present state involves active efforts to counter the rise of Soviet power which may either threaten it directly or, by being successful in Europe, create a situation when China will have to face it without the Soviet Union having a "second front" in Europe.

In this situation the American advances to the Soviet Union cause irritation among Chinese leaders. They look with growing concern at the Soviet-American summit meetings as Chou En-lai made clear in his speech at a banquet for President Nyerere in March 1974. They have shown their disappointment on several occasions. When Dr Kissinger visited Peking in October 1973 not even a common communiqué was produced. Shortly afterwards the heads of the respective diplomatic missions were temporarily withdrawn from Peking and Washington. The visit of Dr Kissinger to Moscow in March 1974 caused another painful reaction on the part of the Chinese leaders. They perceive the American détente policy *vis-à-vis* the Soviet Union as jeopardizing both European and Chinese security interests.

In the wider international context the tilting of the Sino-Soviet balance in favour of the Soviet Union can hardly be in the interest of the United States either.

13

Europe, America and Japan
by Robert A. Scalapino

Two triangular relations are of special importance to the world today. One is the United States-Soviet Union-China relation, vital with respect to war and peace issues of nuclear weapon control, disarmament, and peaceful coexistence. The other is the United States-West Europe-Japan relation, critical to prosperity and development issues, monetary, trade, and investment policies, as well as to the thorny problem of relations between the "advanced" and "emerging" societies.

But both of these three-way relationships pose the most complex difficulties. Communications among the major actors remain limited and strained. Basic policy agreement is exceedingly elusive. Why?

In the U.S.-West European-Japanese triangle, recent history and contemporary trends have interacted to produce several major contradictions. On the one hand, in the immediate aftermath of World War II, remarkable political unity and economic development were achieved in the West and Japan as a result of three factors: desperate needs, a discerned threat, and American largesse.

Organic unity, to be sure, was not achieved, or sought. Relations between West Europe and Japan, indeed, remained quite minimal, with the United States the key link in the overlapping alliance. None the less, basic political and economic trends within the "advanced world" appeared to be relatively uniform.

Today, diversity competes with unity. Nationalism has re-emerged as a vital, possibly dominant force within the so-called advanced world, both in the economic and in the political arena. Contrary to common assumption, moreover, important differences exist in the economic structures of the major industrial societies. Thus the trends may be running as strongly toward economic as toward political multipolarism.

Few would deny that parliamentary democracy faces its most serious crisis since World War II. A combination of economic and social problems threatens to overwhelm a system that has always been recognized as fragile by careful observers.

Contrary to Marxist opinion, most of these problems are not the product of economic stagnation or political repression. On the contrary, they are the result of unprecedented economic growth and new levels of political freedom. It remains true, however, that the current trend is running strongly in the direction of political instability throughout the democratic world. A few months ago, public opinion polls revealed that scarcely a single political leader of the major democratic societies, including Japan, had the support of more than a third of his electorate.

In Western Europe, every government rests upon the narrowest margin of support and challenges to authority and legitimacy loom large. In Japan, the long-time control of the conservative Liberal Democratic party appears threatened, not merely by the growing strength of the opposition, but also by the increasingly deep cleavages within conservative circles.

It is possible that the continuing weaknesses of the opposition, and divisiveness in their ranks, will prolong the status quo. At no time in the post-1945 period, however, have Japanese politics seemed less predictable.

Meanwhile, as is now commonly recognized, the United States faces the gravest problems of internal unity in decades, problems fed by the most bitter administration-media battle in the memory of American citizens.

Under these circumstances, a drift away from international concerns by the population is natural. The vital issues lie close to home—connected with the great changes in life-style which the industrial revolution in its climactic stages is producing. Uncertainty and disillusionment with politics have also led to widespread apathy. Hence the mood at the grass-roots is toward narrowness, not breadth.

At present, popular sentiment in the major democratic states does not support international cooperation, let alone innovation. Rather, the current mood is one of neo-isolationism in the United States, neo-nationalism in Europe and Japan, and protectionism everywhere.

And, in the absence of dynamic, popular leadership, there is no new vision or symbolism to counteract these trends. There is, thus, the danger that even if our political leaders achieve certain technical solutions to current international problems, these solutions will be forced to struggle for survival in a hostile political atmosphere.

Special cultural and political circumstances also pose obstacles. Japan, like Britain, is an island nation lying off a vast continent, and the great historic issue for the two nations has been similar: close cooperation with, or separation from that continent? The answer to this question can never be absolute—nor permanent. Thus, the effort of some Western statesmen to move Japan solidly into "the Atlantic community" can never succeed.

Japan will always remain partly an Asian society despite her deep involvement with the "advanced" industrial world, and her economic-political interests in Asia will probably grow rather than decline in the years immediately ahead.

Meanwhile, the belated European discovery of Japan has been accompanied by strong apprehension. The specter of a yellow industrial peril, justified or not, supports protectionist instincts and restrained contacts. For her part, Japan feels a certain discomfiture in swimming alone in a foreign, white sea —the only non-Western member of an advanced industrial club whose mores and rules remain quasi-foreign.

For these reasons among others, bilateral relations between the United States and Japan, as well as between the United States and Western Europe will continue to be vitally important.

In the economic as in the political sphere, centrifugal tendencies are at work. Contrary to the common impression, the advanced industrial societies are not at the same stage of development at this point. The United States is moving into a phase in which service industries are rapidly increasing in importance at the expense of manufacturing industries. Basic American export capacities now revolve increasingly round two areas: agriculture and high-technology products.

Japan, on the other hand, has the problem of great raw material and energy dependency at a time when hopes continue to rest upon heavy industrial and chemical exports.

Western Europe is closer in these respects to Japan, with the additional complex problem of seeking to advance economic integration via the Common Market in such a manner as to cope with a resurgent political nationalism on the one hand, and to take account of American and Japanese needs on the other.

Given the political and economic trends outlined above, the pressures on behalf of autarchy become understandable. Indeed, certain experts believe that the most realistic prospect for the immediate future is a movement toward economic regionalism, with the United States, West Europe and Japan each becoming powerful centres of economic interaction in its own right.

In considerable degree, this trend has been under way for some time. Economic and political multipolarisms, however, have their limits—both as concepts and as realities. In the political realm, the dominant international tactic today remains balance-of-power politics, as even Russian and Chinese policies illustrate.

In this arena, moreover, there are still only two superpowers, whatever the reduction of their absolute or available power. Thus, for West Europe, two parallel, interrelated issues present themselves: should the two superpowers, and more particularly the Soviet Union, be confronted by separate (and much weaker) states, or should a greater degree of political-military integration within Europe be sought? And should Western Europe continue to lean to one side, preserving its alliance with the United States, or should it move toward "neutralism," on the assumption that ideological-institutional differences and the factor of proximity marking off the Soviet Union and the United States have lost their significance for Europe?

Japan has somewhat different, yet similar alternatives: whether to practice self-sufficiency in political and military matters or even to re-emerge as a political-military power in Asia; continue to rely upon the United States in defense matters; or seek a neutralist stance.

Since all alliances in this era are less tightly knit, more porous, a certain tendency toward more independent, regionally oriented political and military policies—with some "neutralist" quotient—is now under way and this will continue. Neither Western Europe nor Japan, however, is likely to consider the time propitious for an experiment in full-fledged neutralism on the one hand, or total military-political self-sufficiency on the other. Thus, alignment—and competition—with the United States will remain important.

Similarly, in the economic realm, autarchy—single-nation or regional—will be a significant factor in this period of rapidly moving, diversified trends, but it cannot be the all-controlling force. A viable international monetary system, suitable trade and investment policies, and a host of other issues in the economic sphere demand joint efforts on the part of the United States, Western Europe and Japan at this point. But there must also be the clear recognition that such efforts can only be supplements to, not substitutes for, domestic, regional and bilateral policies.

The twin keys to our times are complexity and coordination.

Multitiered approaches to our most basic international issues, political and economic, are essential. But these approaches must be carefully coordinated. In concrete terms, this means that if the work of experts at one level is to be effective, we must find a way to revitalize democratic politics at another level, so that our peoples will be prepared to support rational, complicated international policies. It is in these respects that the United States, Western Europe and Japan share momentous common problems and, let us hope, can find appropriate responses.

14

The Alliance and the Third World

by Irving Brown

No one can contest the primordial objective of NATO stated twenty-five years ago and again reaffirmed on June 10 1974, namely "to protect . . . freedom and independence". In dedicating themselves "to the principles of democracy, respect for human rights, justice and social progress", the Atlantic Treaty countries have once more recognized that the Alliance cannot be conceived in military terms only. This is a clear reaffirmation of Article 2 of the North Atlantic Treaty of 1949 which reads as follows: "The Parties will contribute toward the further development of peaceful and friendly international relations by strengthening their free institutions, by bringing about a better understanding of the principles on which these institutions are founded, and by promoting conditions of stability and well-being. They will seek to eliminate conflict in their international economic policies and will encourage economic collaboration between any or all of them." In effect, this meant that political, economic and social considerations should not be excluded from Alliance planning.

These considerations are especially pertinent in considering the relationships between the highly industrialized NATO nations and the developing countries of the Third World.

The first and most immediate problem involves those nationalist movements still engaged in fighting for freedom, independence and sovereignty, especially those in Portuguese and Southern Africa, which has plagued the Alliance countries ever since the creation of NATO. Thus in the fifties, NATO was accused of helping the colonial powers in the French war with the FLN in Algeria and in recent years similar attacks have been made against NATO for alleged support of Portugal's war in the colonies. This has been highlighted by the recent coup in Portugal and the new government's promise to deal with the problem.

The absence of a positive policy by the Western industrial nations in the post-war years has no doubt contributed considerably to the weakening of the democratic world in dealing with the rising new developing nations. It is regrettable that the Alliance countries did not fully appreciate the importance and significance of the early struggles of the nationalist movements against some of the countries in NATO. For, after all, the organization of NATO was based on the concept of defense against any aggression which interfered with a nation's freedom, independence or sovereignty. The Alliance also affirmed the rights of peoples and nations to self-determination and to defense against any interference through the imposition of military force. This certainly applied to the NATO countries in their relationships with Eastern Europe. And the Soviet action in Czechoslovakia in 1968 re-emphasized this continuing need for defense against aggression and any interference with the sovereignty of other nations.

This raises the question of how to deal with countries that are ruled by various forms of dictatorship and/or colonialism. Western Europe, whether it be NATO or the Common Market, cannot ignore these problems indefinitely. For, if it is right to have an association of free nations organized for the defense of their security and against all forms of external aggression, they must inevitably also consider those internal problems which beset some of their members or those outside their groupings.

In the case of Portugal, there is an exceedingly good opportunity for NATO and other West European or Euro-American organizations to associate themselves with the present Portuguese government which is seeking to end the system of colonialism through an agreement with the independent nationalist movements.

And this, of course, means also that the Western nations should concern themselves with the present dictatorship of Spain as well. For the lesson of Portugal is not only that one cannot and should not ignore movements engaged in fighting for freedom and independence but, equally important, that neglect by the free world to deal with these problems permits the enemies of NATO to exploit the situation in order to become a dominant if not the dominant political factor when independence is achieved.

The failure to appreciate the importance of the national liberation movements in post-war foreign policy formation has contributed much to the decline of the position of the free nations throughout the world. The inability to perceive that the national liberation movements were not originally or necessarily directed against the free world has been a fatal flaw in the calculations of the Western countries, including the United States. For it must be remembered that the philosophical and ideological heritage that we usually associate with Western civilization has been a prime motivating factor among the leaders of most of the nationalist movements throughout the world. In a sense, the ideals of the three great revolutions of America, France and England have given inspiration to most of these leaders, whether in Africa, Asia or Latin America. And it should perhaps be recalled, in this connection, that many of the nationalist leaders have also been ardent opponents of communism, just as the international communist movement has been most wary of nationalism as a political force. This has been true not only in the political field but in the trade unions of many of these countries as well. Thus, most of the nationalist trade union movements in Algeria, Morocco, Tunisia, Vietnam, as well as in Africa, Asia and Latin America, did not join or remain long with the Soviet-controlled world labor movement but did affiliate at one time or another with the free labor forces of the world. And in our opposition to Soviet colonialism, it should be made clear in word and deed that such opposition extends to colonialism in all forms and manifestations.

At the present time, this poses a serious question for the free world in connection with Southern Africa. Unless the free nations, especially the United Kingdom, the United States and all those associated with NATO and the Common Market, re-examine their attitude to the nationalist movements in that part of the world, totalitarian forces may well achieve a preponderant and possibly a dominant influence over the future independent governments there. This is why it would be a mistake for Western leaders to think of Southern Africa in terms of military security only. While Soviet military operations and manoeuvers in the Indian Ocean cannot and should not be ignored, the West can ill afford to remain for long, and at the same time, indifferent to the peoples of these areas and their expectations.

For what will it gain the free world to strengthen its military alliance with an apartheid South Africa and lose the support or confidence of the great masses of Africans who sooner or later will play a decisive role in the future of their countries?

The second, and perhaps long-range consideration, is the problem of relationships with the governments of most of the already independent nations, especially those in Africa where independence has come only in the last ten or fifteen years. The need to deal with this corresponds to the need for both a political and an economic policy of the Atlantic nations toward the developing economies of these countries. Although the Atlantic Alliance is mainly geared toward free world unity and security against possible aggression, one cannot for long ignore the linkage, especially between Africa and Europe, due to the colonial past and present of some of the major European countries. Just as it is essential to give some indication of support or consideration of the need for political independence, the industrialized nations must also give consideration to the need for assisting these less developed countries to achieve economic independence. These economic problems have become extremely serious in recent times due to increasing inflation, rising oil prices and the devastating effects of the drought in many parts of Africa.

It would be tragic if the rich industrial nations were to continue what has become a growing negativism toward the economic and social problems of the developing world. For it must not be forgotten that the industrial world is a small area when we recall that more than two-thirds of the peoples of the world are living in extreme poverty with the highest average annual *per capita* income not more than two hundred dollars. To ignore the economic needs of these nations might well prove disastrous for the future of the West. For, as an experienced British observer and expert on communist warfare has put it: "the strategic concept of revolutionary wars of using 'the countryside of the world' to encircle the 'cities' [North America and Europe] would be several steps nearer fulfilment." It therefore becomes most essential that the Atlantic nations give due regard to the necessity of holding out hope and encouragement to the peoples of these so-called "countryside" areas. In line with the general strategy of defense against aggression, it is vital that serious attention also be given to the kind of indirect aggression going on in the "cities" which reaches its extreme in the form of urban political and/or partisan warfare.

The need for military security, therefore, whether in Europe or the United States, makes it essential to contribute to the creation of a peaceful "city and countryside" situation. To do this effectively, however, the Euro-American Alliance must not only devise an overall economic strategy to assist the poorer nations but also provide a political philosophy and ideological concept to counter what is certainly a growing political threat in those parts of the world. Just as the Marshall Plan in Europe was an assistance program with a concept of a united European economy, so it is necessary in areas like Africa, for instance, to launch a program and a concept which can help both economically and ideologically to guarantee and safeguard a common heritage of freedom, independence and national sovereignty.

15

Defense is Definitely a Two-Way Street

by Georg Leber

"The Europeans are conceited and ungrateful." This at least is the opinion of some Americans. "We helped them to get back on their feet after the Second World War. Today they are our competitors in all parts of the world and on top of it they expect us to defend them."

"The Americans are arrogant and egotistic." This is what some Europeans think. "At the time of the Soviet bloc threat, when they needed us, they courted us. And today they hold us responsible for their problems. They want to withdraw from common defense even though it is their security which is defended in Europe."

In the countries of the Atlantic alliance, not a few black-and-white comments like these could be cited to describe feelings found on both sides of the Atlantic. Although Henry Kissinger pleaded for more cooperation in the "Year of Europe", the "Atlantic River" seems to have widened. In Europe as in America there are people who fancy they could do without their old allies and yet lose nothing.

This is wrong. The political situation calls for a different course of action. The Europeans have to rely upon America even when their economy prospers. For America, independent Western European nations are one of the essentials if, compared with the Soviet Union, it does not want to become a secondary power. Americans and Europeans are sitting in one boat, and therefore we should at least be wise enough to follow the maxim: "Don't rock the boat". The degree of interdependence of political, economic, and social factors which we have to take into account in order to understand our common situation can only be assessed in the larger context of world politics. The European countries of the alliance are, geographically speaking, merely a narrow strip of the huge Eurasian continent. Left alone, they would be in a strategically unfavorable position against the heavily armed Soviet power bloc with its nuclear armament almost equivalent to that of the United States. In spite of its great economic power, Western Europe with its slightly more than 308 million inhabitants is no sufficient counterweight to the highly concentrated and well-disciplined power of the Soviet Union and the other Warsaw Pact nations.

At present, of the NATO forces in Europe, the West European nations contribute ninety per cent of the ground forces, eighty per cent of the naval forces and seventy-five per cent of the air forces. Even if this contribution to our common security were further increased, the Western European nations could not possibly develop into an independent third power, since their security against the Soviet Union can only be guaranteed by an effective alliance with the United States of America. Close ties with the United States, both political and military, alone can guarantee the security and independence of Western Europe.

The undeniable fact therefore remains: Western Europe is America's forward line of defense.

This assessment is the underlying reason why joint efforts to maintain the Atlantic Alliance ties in the future have to be continued and made evident in the day-to-day decisions.

One basis for our security is our economy and it alone can mobilize the resources needed to maintain modern armed forces. The economic capabilities of the NATO countries are much greater than the GNP of the Warsaw Pact countries. This explains why in a phase of détente the Soviet Union is making every effort to reach our levels of performance in the fields of economy, research, and science through cooperation with the West.

In attempts to win major project contracts, ruthless competition among Western nations for the favor of the Soviet Union may have ruinous consequences for all of us.

Tensions in our monetary system and attempts to make profits at the expense of one's partners would in the long run do great harm to our interests. For this reason, the United States and Western Europe must try to find constructive and fair solutions to their trade and currency problems, lest they suffer from a reduction in their level of security.

Nobody can overlook the debates in the United States revolving about the question whether or not to reduce her troops in Europe. However, a decision by the United States to withdraw its troops across the Atlantic Ocean would neatly fit into the Soviet Union's long-term concept of reaping advantages at all levels from the conferences on security and cooperation, thereby strengthening its position of power without any reciprocal concessions. And nothing would be more liable to split Europe and America apart than an American decision in favor of a mere symbolic presence in Europe.

Moreover, the events of recent months have taught us how rapidly crisis situations can develop. If, in times of tension, American troops had to be redeployed to Europe, this would confront the U.S. government with a difficult political decision between the possibilities of failing to move up the necessary reinforcements in time or of escalating a critical situation by early action.

Considering this situation it also appears to be somewhat contradictory for members of the U.S. Congress to advocate unilateral U.S. force reductions on the ground of inadequate financial support—as for instance offset payments to be made by the Federal Republic of Germany—while acknowledging at the same time the great efforts of that country both in support of the U.S. currency and in relieving the burdens of the American military presence in Europe.

It must be said quite clearly that the development of an Atlantic partnership, guaranteeing equitable rights to all its members, would be seriously jeopardized and exposed to great stress by the unilateral reductions in the U.S. military presence in Europe, a decision that would additionally also contravene the common security interests. Likewise, it is equally detrimental to the equal partnership concept when the very basis of Atlantic cooperation, including strategy, is questioned again and again. Even the most elegant formula will not solve Atlantic problems if we lack joint interests and the political will to explore new ways. We should not burn our old existing bridges while plans for new constructions have not at least reached the stage of approval.

The development of Atlantic partnership must be paralleled by efforts towards détente which were initiated by the nuclear test ban, by SALT-1, the agreement of San Clemente on the prevention of nuclear wars, the German federal government's Ostpolitik and the Berlin Four-Powers agreement. A new relationship between East and West can only be achieved gradually. On the long road to normalization of these relations, all steps must be kept under control. We must make good use of our opportunities: if we want to avert the threat jeopardizing both America and Europe, we must have an Atlantic alliance which rests firmly on two sound pillars, America and Europe. Our guiding principles must therefore be:

First, the North Atlantic alliance continues to be the foundation of the security of the Western world. It should be developed to reach a level of genuine partnership between Europe and North America. Changes are needed which will strengthen and not weaken or dissolve our alliance.

Second, the effectiveness of the alliance depends decisively on the transatlantic ties, which must not be weakened; on keeping the elements of foreign policy, economy and defense well-balanced and coordinated among the allies; and on keeping alive among the nations of the Western world the will for self-assertion.

Third, among rival power groups, the balance of military power is the most reliable instrument for maintaining peace in this imperfect world of ours. Power vacuums are the harbingers of crises and wars.

Fourth, in view of the progressive unification of Europe and as a result of successful MBFR negotiations, modifications in the contribution of the United States to this balance may perhaps become possible without endangering the security of the members of our alliance. Any unilateral reductions independent of these developments, however, are bound to lead to crises.

Fifth, continued success in East-West cooperation in various fields, progress in the political integration of Western Europe, and a higher degree of coordination between Europe and the United States will enable us to use for the well-being of our citizens the resources and means now committed to defense without, however, jeopardizing that security which alone guarantees our freedom. This, I feel, is a valid political goal for the years ahead.

16

Security and Defense in the Age of Détente

by Roy Mason

"My government will give full support to the maintenance of the North Atlantic alliance. They will regard the North Atlantic Treaty Organization as an instrument of détente no less than of defense."

I do not for a moment suppose that particular part of the Queen's Speech at the opening of the new Parliament caused too much excitement at home or abroad. The eagerness was for news of the new government's plans on prices, housing, labor relations and so forth. The crucial importance of NATO is one of the few things on which this British government and its predecessor wholeheartedly agree. But I imagine that many of those who did notice this part of the speech, and especially the younger ones, wondered why the North Atlantic alliance was still regarded as so important.

It is inevitable that in NATO's twenty-fifth anniversary year we should look back to the conditions in which the alliance was formed. In 1949, Europe was only just starting to recover from the most ruinous of wars, Germany was disarmed, the danger of Soviet aggression seemed real and immediate. The United

States was unquestionably the most powerful military and economic force in the world.

In the twenty-five years that have gone by Europe has recovered, and gone on to unprecedented prosperity. Germany has built powerful armed forces. The danger of a war in Europe seems remote. The United States and Russia have an effective parity in strategic nuclear weapons. The rise of Europe and Japan as economic powers has profoundly affected U.S. economic interests. Americans have seen the U.S. dollar, once thought the supreme currency, twice devalued.

Furthermore, we have left the sterile polemics of the cold war behind. The Russians are now talking in terms of détente and cooperation. We have constructive discussions proceeding—the Strategic Arms Limitation Talks, the talks on Mutual and Balanced Force Reductions, the Conference on Security and Cooperation in Europe—instead of exchanges of insults. These discussions will be a test of the extent to which the Russians are prepared to recognize the substance as well as the principle of détente.

In this vastly changed situation it is not surprising that the continuing validity of the alliance is questioned by many people. So why does the British government feel that the alliance is still vital as an instrument of defense, and an important tool of détente?

The alliance was formed in response to a threat. That threat may seem to have receded in the new atmosphere of détente. But there is no sign that the Russians, who must want to improve the living standards of their people just as much as we in the West do, are dismantling the powerful forces they maintain at enormous cost.

Soviet military power has increased and is increasing. They have built up a strategic nuclear force to the point where they have parity with the United States. Though, unlike Europe, they do not depend on the world's sea lanes for vital supplies, they have built the second largest battle fleet in the world. Their capacity to enforce their views by the use or threat of the use of force is formidable indeed.

In this situation the ultimate guarantee of Europe's security is America's strategic power. And America knows that if Europe were to fall under Russian domination it would mean a basic shift in the whole world security situation. America's own security would be threatened. As Henry Kissinger said in March this year, "Of course the defense of Europe is also the defense of the United States and we do not have troops in Europe in order to do a favor to the Europeans."

The Europeans already do a great deal in their own defense and have made great efforts to improve their contribution. In the ten years from 1963 to 1973 the European members of the alliance have increased their proportion of NATO countries' defense expenditure from one-quarter to one-third; this is a real shift in relative efforts. The Eurogroup of Defense Ministers, formed after an initiative from Denis Healey, then British Secretary of State for Defense, has played a considerable part in these efforts. In the five years since Eurogroup was formed the total defense budget of its members has almost doubled—from $15.8 billion to $30.2 billion—while that for North America has in fact declined slightly, from $82.5 billion to $80.8 billion.

In 1970 the Eurogroup launched the European Defense Improvement Program, a five-year, $1-billion program of additional defense improvements, now nearly complete. And the momentum of Eurogroup force improvements has been maintained; for instance, in 1973 and 1974 Eurogroup countries will have introduced into service over 800 main battle tanks, over 2,500 other armored vehicles, over 300 modern combat aircraft and 60 or more warships.

The European allies recognize that they must continue to pull their weight in the alliance. But I hope that American public opinion similarly recognizes the considerable, and increasing, extent to which they are already doing so. As the U.S. Secretary of Defense said in his latest annual report: "In fairness, we should acknowledge at the outset that NATO defense has been far from a single-handed effort by the United States. Of the peace-time forces deployed in the European area, our allies contribute approximately ninety per cent of NATO's ground forces, eighty per cent of the ships and seventy-five per cent of the aircraft."

Our alliance must be one of the most successful in history. For twenty-five years we have kept the peace in Europe by sticking together and showing that we can and will fight for our freedom. And it is not just ministers and generals who have worked together; an immense amount of work had been put into the day-to-day tasks. This work is unglamorous, and of course attracts hardly any attention. But it is this work which translates declarations of principle and intent into measures of practical cooperation. We have every reason to be proud of this work.

The MBFR negotiations raise the hope that both East and West may be able to preserve their security in Central Europe at a lower level of forces. It is a tribute both to the cooperative spirit of the NATO allies and to the effectiveness of alliance machinery that, without fuss or polemics, we have reached an agreed negotiating position on MBFR. These negotiations will be long and complex and the building-up of mutual trust and confidence that will be necessary for any negotiated settlement to survive will be a slow process. The NATO allies must continue to work together to ensure Europe's security in the course of negotiations in the same spirit as they work together to defend it by force of arms if necessary. How should they work together? We cannot but admit that the alliance has come under strain in the past year and, while we tend to think of it as a military alliance, it is on economic and political, rather than purely military matters, that our difficulties have arisen. The Americans have felt, and given expression to, disappointment and exasperation with European attitudes on a number of questions. The Europeans in their turn, it seems, have felt the Americans insensitive to their difficulties, and too ready to embark on a course of action without first consulting with their allies. It is time, I think, to pause and take stock. Britain is a European nation and this government will seek a wider cooperation between European peoples.

But we emphatically reject the view that the only way Europe can establish an identity for itself is by constant dissociation of its policies from those of the United States. We see our relations with our American and European allies as complementary, not conflicting.

A great deal of publicity—perhaps too much—has been given to recent disagreements between Europe and America. We must not forget that the issues which unite us are far larger, far more important, than those which divide us. We tend to take our alliance for granted. But its value in preserving our security is one of the fundamental points on which we all agree.

My belief is that NATO will adjust, as it has done before, to the changed economic and political facts of life. We have spent much time—too much—in airing individual differences recently. It is time now to work together in support of our abiding common interests. Only by effective cooperation and consultation between members of the alliance, on economic and political as well as military matters, can we hope to achieve a lasting agreement for Europe's security.

We now have the opportunity, afforded by the MBFR talks, to negotiate security at reduced levels of forces, to reduce tension and to shed some of the crippling armaments burden.

I cannot believe that the NATO allies will fail to win the best possible security arrangements from these negotiations simply because they cannot manage their relations with each other; or that they will fail to look to their defenses until this détente, which we all hope for, has become a reality.

17

NATO's Constant Need—Improvement

by James R. Schlesinger

There has been a recent tendency in the United States to re-examine and to question post-World War II American foreign and defense policy. I welcome and support such an examination. Any policy should be re-examined periodically, and, after Vietnam, we especially needed a new public debate about what our interests are and what they should be.

I feel certain that in any re-examination of the national interests of the United States, the continuation of a viable and secure Atlantic alliance will be reaffirmed as among the most permanent security interests to which we remain committed. It is no doubt true that if the nations of Western Europe were to suffer a fate similar to their eastern neighbours, the United States could, perhaps, survive even though it were isolated in the Western Hemisphere. But we would be living in a world quite different from the one we now know. We would be constrained in ways that would be deeply disturbing to the American people. I have no doubt that the American commitment to European security is, in the view of most Americans, an essential part of American security.

The NATO strategy for maintaining the security of the alliance is deterrence—deterrence across the complete spectrum of risk, from political coercion to all-out nuclear attack. The forces we field to achieve this deterrence form a "NATO triad", comprised of strategic forces (primarily provided by the United States), tactical nuclear forces and a stalwart conventional capability. These forces must form a seamless web, interwoven to provide a credible deterrent against all degrees of coercion or aggression. There must be no gaps in the deterrent —either real or perceived—or the total deterrent will be weakened.

It is precisely to strengthen the deterrent that the United States has recently proposed adjustments in its strategic nuclear-targeting doctrine. Over the years, as Soviet strategic nuclear capabilities have grown, there has been an understandable tendency in Europe to regard the commitment of U.S. strategic forces to Western European security as waning in credibility. The proposed changes in our strategic targeting doctrine provide greater flexibility and selectivity in our targeting, and would permit, in response to a Soviet attack, nuclear options other than the relatively massive options that now exist.

While the NATO triad has consistently included both nuclear and conventional forces, the role of these forces has changed with time. In NATO's early days, the United States enjoyed a clear superiority in nuclear forces which allowed NATO to consider a strategy based on the trip-wire concept, by which the conventional ground forces in Europe would serve primarily to trigger nuclear retaliation by the United States against a Warsaw Pact attack. It was also the case, initially, that there seemed no practical alternative, for the Allied economies were exhausted from the war, Allied armies—much more so than the Soviet armies—had substantially demobilized following the war, and the German forces were nonexistent.

Now that the Soviet Union is reaching nuclear parity with the United States, the value of nuclear weapons in the total deterrent is declining. This clearly does not mean that the American nuclear commitment to the security of the alliance has been outdated. The commitment is firm. But it is clear that the emergence of nuclear parity places a greater value on NATO's conventional military capabilities—not because NATO wishes to wage conventional war, but because we do not wish to wage any war.

NATO conventional forces which can contribute to this balanced deterrent are considerable and are improving in quality. NATO already has sufficient manpower in uniform for a non-nuclear defense and must now turn to making effective use of this manpower and raising the quality of its equipment. Western economies are substantially stronger than in earlier times and are able to sustain—if there is the political will—an adequate defense effort.

The United States, for its part, is maintaining more than 300,000 men in the European area, including over four Army divisions and twenty-seven tactical Air Force squadrons. Two-thirds of another division and seven tactical Air Force squadrons are "dual-based"—i.e., they are stationed in the United States and are available on immediate notice to move to Europe to pre-designated positions. Two additional divisions now in the United States have their equipment prepositioned in Europe and, together with eleven U.S.-based Air Force squadrons, could be as swiftly deployed to Europe as the dual based forces. Still other U.S. land and air forces are available should they be required. At sea, U.S. naval forces are quite powerful and are available to protect, in concert with other NATO navies, our long and relatively exposed sea lanes across the Atlantic and into the Mediterranean.

U.S. ground and air forces are substantially more ready and better equipped than they were five years ago, at the height of the Vietnam war. Furthermore, we are proposing to the Congress a number of important steps which will increase their readiness still further, and allow us to plan on faster deployments of U.S. forces to Europe in an emergency.

The contribution of the European allies is also substantial—and absolutely indispensable if we are to ensure Western security and maintain the essential balance of forces. The European nations provide the bulk of the ready forces in Europe in peacetime: about ninety per cent of the ground forces and seventy-five to eighty per cent of the air and naval forces. The European members of the alliance maintain armed forces totalling over three million men, comprising 56 army divisions plus over 50 regimental units, over 750 combat ships and more than 2,500 aircraft. This is a sizable force.

In combination, therefore, NATO has fielded a very respectable conventional capability. It is true, of course, that NATO forces are in some areas outnumbered by those of the Warsaw Pact. In the vital central region of Europe, the Warsaw Pact ground forces outnumber NATO in deployed manpower 925,000 to 777,000. The Pact also has a substantial superiority in tanks, 15,500 to 6,000 for NATO. It is our intent to reduce any such disparities, and to achieve a more stable balance of forces for the long run. We aim to do this in part through the Mutual and Balanced Force Reduction (MBFR) negotiations now under way in Vienna, and in part through qualitative improvements and closer cooperation among NATO forces.

We thus have in prospect the essential ingredients for effective deterrence and defense, provided—and the proviso is crucial—we in NATO keep up our individual defense efforts. We must also make a greater collective effort to achieve a more efficient and effective use of our resources by integrating our forces more closely within the alliance.

There has been a long-standing concern in Europe that the United States would soon make substantial reductions in its forces in Europe and that this, together with the declining deterrent value attributed to strategic nuclear forces, would detract greatly from Western European security. But American actions have been to the contrary: U.S. forces oriented to NATO have not been reduced. Instead, they are being given the highest priority, their readiness is steadily improving, their equipment is being modernized.

Moreover, there continues to be strong support for NATO in the United States—in the executive branch, in the Congress and among the public—for Americans in general understand the importance to their nation of a free Western Europe. What endangers that support is the continuing belief that the costs associated with European security are not being fairly shared.

The real question for NATO is not whether American forces will be withdrawn. The real question—the answer to which may well help to decide the fate of the West in the decades ahead—is whether the NATO nations will continue to see their interest as best served by working with each other, and whether, with regard to the collective defense effort, there will be a fair sharing of the burden. The recent efforts in NATO to offset the U.S. balance of payments deficit have been helpful.

But, for the longer run, if NATO defense arrangements are to be viable we must see a greater sense of responsibility within the alliance for the sharing of the burden. The proposals for reductions in defense spending now being contemplated in some allied capitals—particularly those which are already spending on defense a relatively modest percentage of their gross national product—run counter to this principle. If reductions in forces, readiness and budgets are to occur anywhere, they can lead only to an unraveling of NATO's defense posture, and in the United States to a serious decline of interest in maintaining forces in Europe, particularly among those who have hitherto been ardent supporters of the NATO presence.

There is a belief in some quarters that the policy of improving relations with the East—the policy of détente—permits NATO nations to make substantial and continuing reductions in defense spending. This is a mistaken assumption. Peaceful, more productive relations are certainly to be sought, and will be greatly welcomed. Indeed, we hope and expect that better relations will in part flow from the Strategic Arms Limitation Talks and MBFR negotiations. But we recognize that the incentive for seeking peaceful relations lies in the Soviet perception of Western strength, and not in our weakness.

If our high hopes for peace are to have solid foundations, and if we are to conduct our political and economic relationships in the world with an ample measure of confidence in our security posture, then NATO countries must continue to maintain a military capability in balance with that of the Warsaw Pact. In seeking this essential balance, we obviously cannot ignore the facts of the Soviet defense effort, however unpleasant those facts may appear. Soviet defense spending since 1960 has risen an average of three per cent per year in real terms (i.e., after inflation). Soviet armed forces have increased by more than one million men—1.5 million by our estimates—in those years. At first, many of these additional forces went to the Soviet-Chinese border; more recently, however, some have gone to Eastern Europe.

It is true that NATO countries have improved the quality of their forces, at least in the last several years. There has been real growth, on the order of ten to twelve per cent, in the defense spending of the European allies from 1970 through 1973, and this spending has been translated into a stronger NATO capability. The United States, for its part, has been steadily improving the quality and readiness of its NATO-oriented forces during this period, despite an overall decline in its budgets (measured in constant dollars) and force structure in the aftermath of Vietnam.

Barring unforeseen circumstances, there is no need for vastly greater NATO defense expenditures in the years ahead. We can achieve and maintain an effective balance of forces provided the NATO countries collectively do not falter in their present defense efforts. We have a common interest in doing so.

18

Is Western Civilization an Obsolete Concept?

by Hugh Trevor-Roper

Western man is distinguished from other men—not only from the less developed peoples but also from the civilizations of India and China—by his sense of history. Having this sense, he periodically seeks to use it to compare and to prophesy. He sees himself standing at a recurrent point of time and looks forward to a recurrent future. Somewhat unaccountably, he seems to do this generally (though not always) when his mood is gloomy, when he thinks that he can look forward to a period not of prosperity but of decline. He is particularly disposed to do so now, when the superpowers seem to overshadow the divided countries of Europe and a new despotism, based on massive technology, seems to threaten those liberties which Europe claims to have discovered. Now at last, it seems, world history is ceasing to be European history, and the whole concept of "Western civilization", which so recently seemed to be firmly established, may become obsolete.

Before considering this argument on its merits, it may be useful to remember that it is not new. In the time of the European Renaissance, when Western civilization was beginning to expand, its dissolution was regularly prophesied. Some expected its doom to be sounded by the Last Trump, others by the Turks. In the 17th century, with the Thirty Years War, the prophets of gloom became more insistent; in the 19th century they became more historical. The German historian Niebuhr at the beginning of the century, the Swiss historian Burckhardt at the end, both saw Europe going through the same process as the Roman Empire in its last convulsions. Since then we have had Spengler and Toynbee. And there are many others.

Once the general parallel has been made, the particular details are easily fitted in. Henry Kissinger recently compared the European states with the Greek cities, unable to unite against the power of Rome. Others have seen Communism as the new ideology which will dissolve the traditions and identity of the West, as Christianity dissolved and replaced the pagan civilization of antiquity.

These parallels may prove to be true. The fact that they have proved false in the past does not mean that they are wrong this time. On the other hand they may well be wrong again. In any case, I believe that they are wrong philosophically. I do not believe that "civilizations" are distinct organisms with a regular life cycle, so that their stages can be predicted like the stages of animal life. Theoretically, a civilization is capable of indefinite prolongation or renewal. In fact, if Western civilization has reached its total term, that will not be because its term has always been fixed: it will be because this time its structure is threatened from without or has been undermined from within.

Unquestionably Western civilization is threatened today. The great technological changes of our time have transformed the nature of political power, and many of the attitudes of the past, which we regard as specifically "Western", now seem out of date. Moreover, the same technological changes have made the European countries, with their distinct, competing societies and traditions, which were the motor of civilization in the past, seem suddenly impotent. If the countries of Western

Europe are the legitimate and necessary custodians of Western civilization, that civilization is today unquestionably weak: weak materially, because they cannot stand up to the power of organized continents; weak morally, because they have lost the self-confidence which they so long enjoyed.

In the past, European liberals—and "liberalism" has always been regarded as the essential character of Western civilization —believed in progress. They believed that they possessed the key to the future and therefore that the future was on their side. Now, looking inwards, at the tensions produced by this century, and outwards, at the more powerful and less "liberal" rivals which seem to threaten them, they find it difficult to continue that belief. The future, it seems, must be with the superpowers; and although, in theory, the superpowers might be the continuators of "Western" civilization, as the Roman Empire continued Greek civilization, we cannot safely make any such assumption. Marxism may be a legitimate development of Western thinking, but Leninism is not. In Russia, Marxism has been distorted beyond recognition. The American experiment seemed, in the past, the triumph of European liberalism, but now that too seems to have become distorted. In both cases, the old tradition has been transformed by objective circumstances: by a historical change in the character of power. The uniform continental power of America or Russia cannot really continue the freedom of Europe, which was linked to the competing pluralism of Europe, any more than the Roman Empire really continued the essential quality of Greek civilization, which was linked to the freedom of the Greek city-states.

The answer to this argument is clear. It is that, since only a continental form of society and government is now viable, Western Europe must itself assume such a form. After all, in resources and population it can rival the continental superpowers. Theoretically there is no reason why it should not turn itself into a superpower too. Economically this is happening already, at least in some respects. And this very process can

be seen as the logical continuation of European history. The last
century saw the unification of Italy and Germany—a process
favored by the "liberals" of the time. That unification was both
economic and political: The minuscule principalities of the 18th
century had proved inadequate, and Napoleon had shown the
way. Napoleon's French imperialism had been defeated, but
after its defeat, other ways were found. In this century, under
the pressure of the new industrialism, even these united countries have proved inadequate, as Hitler showed. But may not
the convulsions of the 20th century, now that we have defeated
our latest tyrannical unifier, lead naturally to a united Europe
which will be the only authentic guarantee of the survival of its
own Western form of civilization?

Against this it may be said that a Europe united both
politically and economically, though viable as a third (or
fourth) superpower, would attain its viability at a heavy price,
for it would itself be a repudiation of typical Western civilization, which is essentially linked to certain forms of government,
a certain philosophy. Liberals, who claim to be the only true
representatives of the "West", insist that that government and
philosophy are liberal.

In fact, I do not believe that this is true. There are many
non-liberal elements in "Western" history, just as there were
monarchies, oligarchies and tyrants as well as democracies in
ancient Greece. Indeed, European "liberalism" is the result of
continuous internal differences, and to that extent owes its
being to non-liberal forces: the professed liberals, if un-
challenged, would have been as illiberal as anyone. The
essential quality of European civilization, I believe, is not one
particular political or philosophical tradition, but its variety:
a variety which has led to struggle and war but has also, by
continuous interplay, created a continuing tradition (which
intellectuals have afterward simplified) and prevented such
stagnation as periodically overcame the other great civilization
of China. As Gibbon wrote, in the 18th century, "the division
of Europe into a number of independent states, connected
however with each other by the general resemblance of religion,
language and manners, is productive of the most beneficial

consequences to the liberty of mankind." To me, one of the great questions of European unity is, how much of that beneficial variety, so essential to Western civilization, can be retained under that economic and political unification which is necessary to its survival?

Admittedly, it is a real problem. Inevitably the creation of a single market in Europe will lead to a certain uniformity and to the opportunities of vast and dangerous patronage, which can weaken independent forces. If Europe should ever have a single central government controlling a unified patronage, I should tremble for the survival of the European inheritance. But I can see alternative possibilities. In a federal structure, preserving distinct authorities and separate systems—what De Gaulle called a *Europe des patries*—I can see the means of preserving European variety even in European unity. For that variety is not artificial. It has deep historic roots. It is precisely because of their depth that European rivalries have been so endemic in the past. Those rivalries are no longer tolerable in their old form; but they can, perhaps, discover a new form. At least it is on such a prospect, not on the naïve belief that there is a distinct "Western" tradition of "liberalism" which must be kept pure and undefiled, that the survival of our form of civilization must depend.

19

Atlantic Differences and Détente
by Joseph Godson

It is symbolic perhaps of the present difficulties in the Atlantic Alliance that, twenty-five years after its birth, members of NATO were unable to agree on a proper way to celebrate the anniversary last spring.

In order, however, to avoid the temptation to exaggerate the current strains and stresses we must not fail to appreciate that since the creation of the Alliance the international system has undergone profound changes. For one thing, the sharp tension between East and West and our fear of military aggression have receded. In deterring aggression and abating tensions the Alliance has indeed been a major success. For another, the very relaxation of tensions has posed serious problems for the West; for the changed international climate has reduced the pressure for unity and has made it easier for centrifugal and divisive forces to assert themselves. In domestic politics, in particular, real or imagined détente has made it more difficult to maintain sufficient national defense capabilities, the appropriations for which are seen increasingly as competing with domestic needs. This presents a constant threat to European-

American diplomacy, which must be based on gradualism and reciprocity in promoting change with the East.

Moreover, the decreased pressure for political and ideological unity in the wake of détente unleashes a variety of potentially destabilizing social forces and, unless a coordinated effort to guide prudently the so-called process of change is made, détente may well lead to new crises.

While military aggression continues to remain a possibility for which NATO must at all times be prepared, the probability of security crises has seriously shifted from direct aggression to types of threat in which external political pressure and blackmail are likely to be more frequent than the overt use of military force. Contrary to growing beliefs, these developments make a coordinated Western security policy more, and not less, imperative.

In this context, bilateral negotiations between the United States and the Soviet Union could be useful, if handled skillfully, without diplomatic hocus-pocus and with proper consultation, in reducing the risks of war and thereby benefit international stability. Above all, it is most essential that America avoid the slightest impression that the two superpowers are acting over the heads and at the expense of the West Europeans. Settlements which appear to exclude member nations and disregard their essential security interests are bound to erode mutual confidence in European-American relations. Indeed, the role of the Alliance in European-American affairs is most essential for providing the degree of political cohesion which is the indispensable condition for détente diplomacy, including specifically the current series of discussions with the Soviet Union and its allies on European security and cooperation, SALT-2, and mutual and balanced force reductions.

Despite this need for political cohesion, however, acrimony and controversies in the field of trade, investment and monetary relations reflect the fact, it would seem, that the countries of Western Europe and North America have to date not developed

an effective system of international management of the highly
interdependent economies of the industrialized world. The
strains caused by disagreements over economic arrangements,
as well as by political and defense issues, have led in recent
months to a serious weakening of European-American relations
and to an erosion, to some degree, of public support on both
sides of the Atlantic for close ties between Western Europe and
the United States.

Henry Kissinger has summed up the difference between the
European and the American approach by claiming that
whereas the United States has global interests, Western Europe
has only regional interests. Another way of putting it is that
there has been some imprecision in the North Atlantic Treaty
from the very beginning. One of its key clauses pledges the
signatories to consider an armed attack against one as an
attack against all, "to be met by such action as each of them
deems necessary, including the use of armed force, to restore
and maintain the security of the North Atlantic area". Leaving
aside the quite important questions of how one defines an
armed attack, or what happens when members disagree on
what is deemed necessary, how is one to define the North
Atlantic area in an era when the range of a submarine-launched
—and therefore eminently movable—ballistic missile is about
6,000 miles? One answer might be that it requires a power of
global capabilities to defend powers whose interests are only
regional or, again, perhaps one of the best ways of defending the
North Atlantic area is from submarines in the Indian Ocean.

Europeans, though, have not become reconciled to this
widening of the area of potential conflict which dependence on
a superpower implies. Equally, they have found no substitute
for reliance on the American strategic deterrent and in what is
known as an era of détente they have tended to reduce their
own ability either to defend themselves or to strengthen the
Alliance.

Meanwhile, congressional pressures for the withdrawal of
substantial numbers of U.S. troops from Europe have increased
to the point where most European leaders believe that a cut-
back will eventually take place. Far from raising their own

force levels to fill the gap, the Europeans are making their own cuts. At the same time, the Soviet Union has gained something very close to nuclear parity with the United States: it is on the way to becoming a global sea power and it continues to increase its firepower in Central Europe. On top of that, the members of the Atlantic Alliance have been quarreling among themselves, and in the East-West MBFR negotiations there is no sign of any progress which would not tilt the balance further in Moscow's favor.

On the Soviet side there is inordinate ambition, which, according to Professor Leonard Schapiro of the London School of Economics, "has always taken the form of expanding wherever and whenever this can be done without risk".

In such a situation, the very survival of the "free world" depends on West European unity and on close cooperation between Europe and America—if only to stop the Soviet Union from exploiting new isolationism in the United States and European divisions and insularity in order to weaken the fabric of NATO.

Both Western Europe and America know that if the Alliance fell to pieces they would be in great peril. Peril of what? Of seeing the triumph in the world of a form of government and a philosophy which denies human freedom, in every field—political, moral and intellectual. This is what makes it worthwhile for America to accept much of its overseas expenditure and for Europe to recognize its nuclear dependence—the fact that they share a common belief in freedom. In today's world, beliefs about freedom and right and wrong are the only things worth fighting for, and the only sure basis for alliances.

But if the Europeans must become more realistic in terms of alliance responsibilities so must the Americans. Both Mr Kissinger and some of his European counterparts must stop perceiving détente as the only alternative to nuclear war. This false alternative provided in the past the underlying premise for those advocating unilateral Western disarmament and is used today by some Western government spokesmen to justify an attitude of silent indifference toward dissenters and victims of Soviet persecution. In fact, the determination to avoid nuclear conflict had characterized the policy of America and the Soviet Union for many years before talk of détente became fashionable—the first instance was the Cuban confrontation of 1962, and the latest example is the worldwide U.S. alert in October, 1973.

Much significance, in this connection, lies in the different interpretations of détente in the West and in the East, which in no small degree add to suspicion and friction inside the Alliance and between its members. To start with, the Soviet concept of peaceful coexistence and détente has little in common with the Western goal of constructive cooperation, and Western proposals for freer exchange of ideas and information as part of the promotion of security, cooperation and détente are described by the Soviets as "ideological subversion", constituting an attempt to return to the cold war.

In a recently-completed 14,000-word all-embracing evaluation of détente by a group of eminent British and American scholars and writers, which included Leonard Schapiro, Richard Pipes, Gregory Crossman, Leopold Labedz, John Erickson, Robert Conquest, Edward Shils, Bernard Lewis, Brian Crozier, P. J. Vatikiotis and this writer, it is stated: "In the present Soviet terminology détente or 'peaceful coexistence' denotes a strategic alternative to overtly militant antagonism against the so-called 'capitalist countries.' It does not imply the abandonment by the Soviet Union and its allies of conflict with the liberal Western countries. It does not mean the cessation of the slogans about class warfare and about the 'ideological' conflict between the 'two systems' with the aim of replacing the capitalist (democratic) system by the communist system. The point is emphatically and repeatedly made in Soviet theoretical pronouncements intended for consumption within the Communist bloc. Détente means a change of methods. Head-on conflict is to yield to indirect methods of combat, using nonmilitary means, described as 'ideological': in Soviet practice this term covers subversion, propaganda, political blackmail and intelligence operations."

Indeed, the Soviet leadership makes no secret of the fact that its opposition to Western ideas and to any significant "liberalization" inside its borders is total and irreconcilable. Such an unrelenting attitude is incompatible with any development of real progress to genuinely friendly relations between the two sides. Until "liberalization" takes place, or until, at least, there are some signs of serious progress in that direction, we are entitled to take all the other elements in détente in current Soviet policy as temporary and tactical in nature.

A genuine détente is, of course, most desirable, but in its present form it has unfortunately proved to be an instrument in the process of weakening the West, as it has succeeded in hiding from it the political and military realities of the situation and lowered the threshold of the risks from the Soviet Union. As the above-mentioned détente study puts it: "It made possible the presentation in the West of political failures as successes for peace, of businessmen's fantasies about profits as rational enterprises in the interests of the state, of Western military decline as an achievement leading towards strategic stability. It is time for the West to recover its sense of reality if Western civilization is to survive."

Meanwhile, let us hope that the picture of political disunity, both within Europe, and between Europe and America, which can only gladden the hearts of their adversaries, will soon come to an end. As British Foreign Secretary James Callaghan put it in Brussels on June 4: "Consultation, cooperation and coordination between Europe and the United States should be as natural as breathing". There is little doubt that the Atlantic countries—joined with Japan—possess hitherto unimagined human material, technical and scientific resources as well as the capability to influence the course of the world to desirable ends. The challenge is to mobilize our capabilities and to enlist the skills and enthusiasms of all our peoples. The task of political far-sighted leadership in the free democratic societies is to recognize the realities, to articulate the common interests, and to inspire a renewed sense of community and purpose.

Appendix A
The North Atlantic Treaty
Washington D.C., April 4 1949*

The Parties to this Treaty reaffirm their faith in the purposes and principles of the Charter of the United Nations and their desire to live in peace with all peoples and all Governments.

They are determined to safeguard the freedom, common heritage and civilization of their peoples, founded on the principles of democracy, individual liberty and the rule of law.

They seek to promote stability and well-being in the North Atlantic area.

They are resolved to unite their efforts for collective defense and for the preservation of peace and security.

They therefore agree to this North Atlantic Treaty:

ARTICLE I

The Parties undertake, as set forth in the Charter of the United Nations, to settle any international dispute in which they may be involved by peaceful means in such a manner that inter-

---

* The Treaty came into force on August 24 1949, after the deposition of the ratifications of all signatory states.

national peace and security and justice are not endangered, and to refrain in their international relations from the threat or use of force in any manner inconsistent with the purposes of the United Nations.

ARTICLE 2

The Parties will contribute toward the further development of peaceful and friendly international relations by strengthening their free institutions, by bringing about a better understanding of the principles upon which these institutions are founded, and by promoting conditions of stability and well-being. They will seek to eliminate conflict in their international economic policies and will encourage economic collaboration between any or all of them.

ARTICLE 3

In order more effectively to achieve the objectives of this Treaty, the Parties, separately and jointly, by means of continuous and effective self-help and mutual aid, will maintain and develop their individual and collective capacity to resist armed attack.

ARTICLE 4

The Parties will consult together whenever, in the opinion of any of them, the territorial integrity, political independence or security of any of the Parties is threatened.

ARTICLE 5

The Parties agree that an armed attack against one or more of them in Europe or North America shall be considered an attack against them all, and consequently they agree that, if such an armed attack occurs, each of them, in exercise of the right of individual or collective self-defense recognized by Article 51 of the Charter of the United Nations, will assist the Party or Parties so attacked by taking forthwith, individually and in concert with the other Parties, such action as it deems necessary, including the use of armed force, to restore and maintain the security of the North Atlantic area.

Any such armed attack and all measures taken as a result thereof shall immediately be reported to the Security Council. Such measures shall be terminated when the Security Council has taken the measures necessary to restore and maintain international peace and security.

ARTICLE 6*

For the purpose of Article 5, an armed attack on one or more of the Parties is deemed to include an armed attack
—on the territory of any of the Parties in Europe or North America, on the Algerian Departments of France**, on the territory of Turkey or on the islands under the jurisdiction of any of the Parties in the North Atlantic area north of the Tropic of Cancer;
—on the forces, vessels, or aircraft of any of the Parties, when in or over these territories or any other area in Europe in which occupation forces of any of the Parties were stationed on the date when the Treaty entered into force or the Mediterranean Sea of the North Atlantic area north of the Tropic of Cancer.

ARTICLE 7

This Treaty does not affect, and shall not be interpreted as affecting, in any way the rights and obligations under the Charter of the Parties which are members of the United Nations, or the primary responsibility of the Security Council for the maintenance of international peace and security.

---

* As amended by Article 2 of the Protocol to the North Atlantic Treaty on the accession of Greece and Turkey.

** On January 16 1963, the French Representative made a statement to the North Atlantic Council on the effects of the independence of Algeria on certain aspects of the North Atlantic Treaty. The Council noted that in so far as the former Algerian Departments of France were concerned the relevant clauses of this Treaty had become inapplicable as from July 3 1962.

ARTICLE 8

Each Party declares that none of the international engagements now in force between it and any other of the Parties or any third State is in conflict with the provisions of this Treaty, and undertakes not to enter into any international engagement in conflict with this Treaty.

ARTICLE 9

The Parties hereby establish a Council, on which each of them shall be represented to consider matters concerning the implementation of this Treaty. The Council shall be so organized as to be able to meet promptly at any time. The Council shall set up such subsidiary bodies as may be necessary; in particular it shall establish immediately a defense committee which shall recommend measures for the implementation of Articles 3 and 5.

ARTICLE 10

The Parties may, by unanimous agreement, invite any other European State in a position to further the principles of this Treaty and to contribute to the security of the North Atlantic area to accede to this Treaty. Any State so invited may become a party to the Treaty by depositing its instrument of accession with the Government of the United States of America. The Government of the United States of America will inform each of the Parties of the deposit of each such instrument of accession.

ARTICLE 11

This Treaty shall be ratified and its provisions carried out by the Parties in accordance with their respective constitutional processes. The instruments of ratification shall be deposited as soon as possible with the Government of the United States of America, which will notify all the other signatories of each deposit. The Treaty shall enter into force between the States which have ratified it as soon as the ratifications of the majority of the signatories, including the ratifications of Belgium, Canada, France, Luxembourg, the Netherlands, the United

Kingdom and the United States, have been deposited and shall come into effect with respect to other States on the date of the deposit of their ratifications.

ARTICLE 12

After the Treaty has been in force for ten years, or at any time thereafter, the Parties shall, if any of them so requests, consult together for the purpose of reviewing the Treaty, having regard for the factors then affecting peace and security in the North Atlantic area including the development of universal as well as regional arrangements under the Charter of the United Nations for the maintenance of international peace and security.

ARTICLE 13

After the Treaty has been in force for twenty years, any Party may cease to be a Party one year after its notice of denunciation has been given to the Government of the United States of America, which will inform the Governments of the other Parties of the deposit of each notice of denunciation.

ARTICLE 14

This Treaty, of which the English and French texts are equally authentic, shall be deposited in the archives of the Government of the United States of America. Duly certified copies will be transmitted by that Government to the Governments of the other signatories.

Appendix B

Declaration on Atlantic Relations

Issued in Ottawa, June 19 1974

1 The members of the North Atlantic Alliance declare that the Treaty signed 25 years ago to protect their freedom and independence has confirmed their common destiny. Under the shield of the Treaty, the allies have maintained their security, permitting them to preserve the values which are the heritage of their civilization and enabling Western Europe to rebuild from its ruins and lay the foundations of its unity.
2 The members of the Alliance reaffirm their conviction that the North Atlantic Treaty provides the indispensable basis for their security, thus making possible the pursuit of détente. They welcome the progress that has been achieved on the road towards détente and harmony among nations, and the fact that a conference of 35 countries of Europe and North America is now seeking to lay down guidelines designed to increase security and cooperation in Europe. They believe that until circumstances permit the introduction of general, complete and controlled disarmament, which alone could provide genuine security for all, the ties uniting them must be maintained. The allies share a common desire to reduce the burden

of arms expenditure on their peoples. But states that wish to preserve peace have never achieved this aim by neglecting their own security.

3 The members of the Alliance reaffirm that their common defense is one and indivisible. An attack on one or more of them in the area of application of the Treaty shall be considered an attack against them all. The common aim is to prevent any attempt by a foreign power to threaten the independence or integrity of a member of the Alliance. Such an attempt would not only put in jeopardy the security of all members of the Alliance but also threaten the foundations of world peace.

4 At the same time they realize that the circumstances affecting their common defense have profoundly changed in the last ten years: the strategic relationship between the United States and the Soviet Union has reached a point of near equilibrium. Consequently, although all the countries of the Alliance remain vulnerable to attack, the nature of the danger to which they are exposed has changed. The Alliance's problems in the defense of Europe have thus assumed a different and more distinct character.

5 However, the essential elements in the situation which gave rise to the Treaty have not changed. While the commitment of all the allies to the common defense reduces the risk of external aggression, the contribution to the security of the entire Alliance provided by the nuclear forces of the United States based in the United States as well as in Europe and by the presence of North American forces in Europe remains indispensable.

6 Nevertheless, the Alliance must pay careful attention to the dangers to which it is exposed in the European region, and must adopt all measures necessary to avert them. The European members who provide three-quarters of the conventional strength of the Alliance in Europe, and two of whom possess nuclear forces capable of playing a deterrent role of their own contributing to the overall strengthening of the deterrence of the Alliance, undertake to make the necessary contribution to maintain the common defense at a level capable of deterring and if necessary repelling all actions directed against the independence and territorial integrity of the members of the Alliance.

7 The United States, for its part, reaffirms its determination not to accept any situation which would expose its allies to external political or military pressure likely to deprive them of their freedom, and states its resolve, together with its allies, to maintain forces in Europe at the level required to sustain the credibility of the strategy of deterrence and to maintain the capacity to defend the North Atlantic area should deterrence fail.

8 In this connection the member states of the Alliance affirm that as the ultimate purpose of any defense policy is to deny to a potential adversary the objectives he seeks to attain through an armed conflict, all necessary forces would be used for this purpose. Therefore, while reaffirming that a major aim of their policies is to seek agreements that will reduce the risk of war, they also state that such agreements will not limit their freedom to use all forces at their disposal for the common defense in case of attack. Indeed, they are convinced that their determination to do so continues to be the best assurance that war in all its forms will be prevented.

9 All members of the Alliance agree that the continued presence of Canadian and substantial U.S. forces in Europe plays an irreplaceable role in the defense of North America as well as of Europe. Similarly the substantial forces of the European allies serve to defend Europe and North America as well. It is also recognized that the further progress towards unity, which the member states of the European community are determined to make, should in due course have a beneficial effect on the contribution to the common defense of the Alliance of those of them who belong to it. Moreover, the contributions made by members of the Alliance to the preservation of international security and world peace are recognized to be of great importance.

10 The members of the Alliance consider that the will to combine their efforts to ensure their common defense obliges them to maintain and improve the efficiency of their forces and that each should undertake, according to the role that it has assumed in the structure of the Alliance, its proper share of the burden of maintaining the security of all. Conversely, they take the view that in the course of current or future negotiations nothing must be accepted which could diminish this security.

11 The allies are convinced that the fulfilment of their common aims requires the maintenance of close consultation, cooperation and mutual trust, thus fostering the conditions necessary for defense and favourable for détente, which are complementary. In the spirit of the friendship, equality and solidarity which characterize their relationships, they are firmly resolved to keep each other fully informed and to strengthen the practice of frank and timely consultations by all means which may be appropriate on matters relating to their common interests as members of the Alliance, bearing in mind that these interests can be affected by events in other areas of the world. They wish also to ensure that their essential security relationship is supported by harmonious political and economic relations. In particular they will work to remove sources of conflict between their economic policies and to encourage economic cooperation with one another.

12 They recall that they have proclaimed their dedication to the principles of democracy, respect for human rights, justice and social progress, which are the fruits of their shared spiritual heritage and they declare their intention to develop and deepen the application of these principles in their countries. Since these principles, by their very nature, forbid any recourse to methods incompatible with the promotion of world peace, they reaffirm that the efforts which they make to preserve their independence, to maintain their security and to improve the living standards of their peoples exclude all forms of aggression against anyone, are not directed against any other country, and are designed to bring about the general improvement of international relations. In Europe, their objective continues to be the pursuit of understanding and cooperation with every European country. In the world at large, each allied country recognizes the duty to help the developing countries. It is in the interest of all that every country benefit from technical and economic progress in an open and equitable world system.

13 They recognize that the cohesion of the Alliance has found expression not only in cooperation among their governments, but also in the free exchange of views among the elected representatives of the peoples of the Alliance. Accordingly, they declare their support for the strengthening of links among parliamentarians.

14 The members of the Alliance rededicate themselves to the aims and ideals of the North Atlantic Treaty during this year of the twenty-fifth anniversary of its signature. The member nations look to the future, confident that the vitality and creativity of their peoples are commensurate with the challenges which confront them. They declare their conviction that the North Atlantic Alliance continues to serve as an essential element in the lasting structure of peace they are determined to build.

Authors

DR. JOSEPH LUNS, Secretary-General of NATO since 1971, served as Minister of Foreign Affairs of The Netherlands from 1953–1971. He holds numerous foreign orders and degrees and has written many articles on foreign affairs in "International Affairs", "La Revue Politique", and others.

MICHAEL STEWART was the British Secretary of State for Foreign Affairs in 1965–66 and the Secretary of State of Foreign and Commonwealth Affairs in 1968–1970. He is also former Secretary of State for Education and Science (1964–65) and the author of "The British Approach to Politics" (1938) and "Modern Forms of Government" (1959).

PIERRE HARMEL is a former Prime Minister (1965–66) and Foreign Minister (1966–1973) of Belgium. He is at present President of the Belgian Senate and Professor of Law at the University of Liège.

J. ROBERT SCHAETZEL was the U.S. Ambassador to the European Community between 1966 and 1972 after having served as Deputy Assistant Secretary of State for Atlantic Affairs in the Department of State.

ANTONIO GIOLITTI is the Italian Minister of Budget and Economic Planning.

HENRY H. FOWLER is a former U.S. Secretary of the Treasury, 1965–68, during the Johnson administration. He is now chairman of the Atlantic Council of the United States and partner of Goldman, Sachs and Company in New York.

J. E. HARTSHORN is a writer and consultant on international oil and energy problems, associated with Walter J. Levy SA of Zug Switzerland. He is the author of "Oil Companies and Governments", and has in preparation a book on "Europe and World Energy".

EMILIO G. COLLADO is chairman of the Business and Industry Advisory Committee to the OECD and executive vice-president of Exxon. He is also a former U.S. Assistant Secretary of State for Economic Affairs.

LANE KIRKLAND is the Secretary-Treasurer of the American Federation of Labor-Congress of Industrial Organisations (AFL-CIO).

BERNARD LEWIS, Professor of History of the Near and Middle East, University of London, since 1949, has written extensively on Islam and the Arab world. Among his books are "The Emergence of Modern Turkey", "The Middle East and the West", "The Assassins" and "Race and Colour in Islam".

EUGENE V. ROSTOW is a Professor of Law at Yale University, President of the Atlantic Treaty Association, and was the U.S. Under-Secretary of State for Political Affairs in

1966–69. He is the author among other works of "A National Policy for the Oil Industry" (1948), "Planning for Freedom" (1959), and "Peace in the Balance" (1972).

LEONARD SCHAPIRO is Professor of Political Science, with special reference to Russian studies, at the London School of Economics and Political Science, University of London. He was in practice at the bar from 1932 to 1955. His books include "The Origins of the Communist Autocracy", "The Communist Party of the Soviet Union", and "Totalitarianism".

LEOPOLD LABEDZ is the editor of "Survey", a quarterly journal of East and West studies, published in London. He has been a visiting Professor at Stanford University since 1971 and is a member of the Advisory Board of "Encounter" magazine. His books include "Revisionism" (1961), "The Sino-Soviet Rift" (1967), and "Solzhenitsyn, a Documentary Record".

ROBERT A. SCALAPINO is Professor of Political Science, University of California, Berkeley, and editor of "Asian Survey". He is the author of numerous books and articles on Asia, among which the most recent are "Asia and the Major Powers" (1972), "Elites in the People's Republic of China" (Editor and contributor to) (1972) and "Communism in Korea", 2 vols. (co-author) (1972).

IRVING BROWN is the AFL-CIO representative in Europe and former Executive Director of the African-American Labor Center.

GEORG LEBER is the West German Minister of Defense and a former Minister of Transport. Before joining the government, he was for many years President of the Building and Construction Workers Union in West Germany.

ROY MASON is the British Secretary of State for Defense. He

was formerly Minister of Power (1968–69) and President of the Board of Trade (1969–70). From 1947–53 he was an official of the National Union of Mineworkers.

JAMES R. SCHLESINGER is the American Secretary of Defense. He is also a former Chairman of the U.S. Atomic Energy Commission. Earlier he served as a teaching fellow in economics and the social sciences at Harvard University and as associate professor at the University of Virginia. He is the author of "Political Economy of National Security" (1960) and co-author of "Issues in Defense Economics" (1969).

HUGH TREVOR-ROPER has been Regius Professor of Modern History at Oxford University since 1957. He is the author of many works, including "The Last Days of Hitler" (1947), "Historical Essays" (1957), "The Rise of Christian Europe" (1965), "The Reformation and Social Change" (1967), "The Philby Affair" (1968), and "The Plunder o the Arts in the Seventeenth Century" (1970).

JOSEPH GODSON was for 21 years a senior Foreign Service Officer with the U.S. State Department, specializing in political and labor affairs. Since his retirement in 1971 he has been living in London doing freelance writing for "The Glasgow Herald", "The Observer", "Socialist Commentary" and the "International Herald Tribune". Last year he organized the Europe-America Conference in Amsterdam.